CONTENTS

Deregulation: The Good and Bad of Cutting Red Tape	1
Chapter 1: The Rise of Deregulation	5
Chapter 2: Transformations in Air Travel	21
Chapter 3: Shifting Landscapes in Telecommunications	38
Chapter 4: Financial Sector's New Frontiers	56
Chapter 5: Energy Market Dynamics	72
Chapter 6: Reshaping the Trucking Industry	89
Chapter 7: Evolution of Cable Television	105
Chapter 8: Competition's Double-Edged Sword	120
Chapter 9: Unintended Outcomes	138
Chapter 10: The Future of Balance	153

DEREGULATION: THE GOOD AND BAD OF CUTTING RED TAPE

By

Emma Powell

"I was an advocate of the deregulation movement and I made - along with a lot of other smart people - a fundamental mistake, which is that deregulation works fine in industries which do not pervade the economy. The financial industry undergirded the entire economy and if it is made riskier by deregulation and collapses in widespread bankruptcies as what happened in 2008, the entire economy freezes because it runs

on credit."
   --Anonymous

Introduction

Understanding Deregulation: A Double-Edged Sword

In 2008, the world watched as financial markets crumbled, triggering a global economic crisis. This catastrophic event, rooted in part in the deregulation of the banking sector, serves as a stark reminder of the power and peril of reduced government oversight.

Deregulation, the process of removing or reducing state regulations, has shaped industries and economies for decades. From the airline industry's transformation in the 1970s to the ongoing debates in environmental policy, the impact of deregulation touches every aspect of our lives.

This book explores the intricate dance between freedom and control in modern economies. We'll examine how deregulation can spark innovation, reduce costs, and drive efficiency. Yet, we'll also confront its dark side: market failures, exploitation, and systemic risks that can threaten entire economies.

As we journey through various sectors – telecommunications, finance, energy, and more – we'll unpack key concepts like market stability, public welfare, and the role of oversight. We'll analyze historical turning points and contemporary case studies, offering a nuanced view of deregulation's effects.

Whether you're a policymaker, business leader, or curious citizen, this book aims to equip you with the knowledge to navigate the complex landscape of deregulation. As we stand at the crossroads of technological revolution and global economic shifts, understanding these dynamics is more crucial than ever.

Join us as we unravel the paradoxes of deregulation and question its place in shaping our economic future. Are we striking the right balance between market freedom and public protection? Let's find out.

CHAPTER 1: THE RISE OF DEREGULATION

Economic Context and Motivation

The late 20th century was a time of economic struggle and dissatisfaction, creating a perfect environment for the ideas of deregulation to take hold. High inflation rates surged like wildfire, fueled by the oil crises of the 1970s. Prices shot up, eating away at the purchasing power of everyday people, while wages remained stagnant, leaving many wondering if the systems meant to help them were actually doing their jobs. Economists started calling this troubling period "stagflation," a term that combined stagnation and inflation, signaling a major failure in traditional economic approaches.

In this atmosphere, Milton Friedman emerged as a leading figure from the Chicago School of Economics. With his captivating arguments and plenty of evidence, he promoted the idea of free-market capitalism. He believed that the government's heavy regulations were often the root of many economic problems. Friedman's ideas struck a chord during a time when people were beginning to doubt the benefits of government intervention. Many felt that the regulations intended to protect consumers were actually restricting the economy they were meant to save. The prevailing view shifted towards the belief that less government oversight would lead to more economic freedom, innovation, and prosperity.

As debates about the balance of state versus market heated up, the political landscape started to evolve. A new era was dawning, one marked by the rise of neoliberal policies that prioritized market forces in economic decision-making. Politicians began to embrace the idea that deregulation was not just necessary for economic growth, but also a moral imperative, freeing the spirit of entrepreneurship and creativity. They argued that the market could regulate itself if given the freedom to operate without constraints.

Major legislative changes emerged, dramatically reshaping the rules that governed industries. For example, the Airline Deregulation Act of 1978 aimed to eliminate government control over fares and routes, allowing airlines to compete freely. This act was celebrated as a significant turning point, with supporters claiming it would lead to lower prices and more options for consumers. Who wouldn't want cheaper flights and more choices? But critics quickly pointed out the downsides—fluctuating airfares and a two-tier system where only the most financially savvy travelers really benefited from this new freedom.

The arguments for deregulation were enticing. Advocates painted a picture of a thriving economy, bursting with innovation and efficiency, where consumers held the power to shape market dynamics. However, beneath this shiny surface lay complex issues that would unfold in the years to come. Many were skeptical about whether deregulation was the miracle cure it was promoted to be. Concerns about safety standards, worker protections, and the risk of monopolies rising without oversight began to surface. As the balance tipped toward a more hands-off approach, the debate intensified, setting the stage for ongoing discussions about the need for regulation versus the benefits of free-market principles.

Society's attitudes shifted alongside these economic theories and political movements. Distrust in the government reached new heights, with many citizens seeing regulations as not just an annoyance, but a significant barrier to progress. Public opinion reflected a growing belief that government actions stifled competition and innovation, rallying support for the deregulation cause. This cultural shift inspired a "let's do it ourselves" attitude, capturing the imaginations of entrepreneurs, investors, and everyday people alike.

It's also important to consider the global backdrop against which these changes were taking place. Countries worldwide were grappling with the challenges of globalization, with businesses competing for an edge in an increasingly connected economy. International trade pressures began to influence domestic markets, pushing nations to rethink their regulatory approaches. Staying competitive on a global level became a rallying cry for deregulation. Countries with strict regulations faced the risk of falling behind, prompting leaders to push for a more market-friendly environment.

The stage was set for a wave of deregulation that would sweep through various sectors, from telecommunications to finance. Policymakers embraced the belief that market forces could deliver the best outcomes for society. As the call for deregulation grew louder, it became clear that the effects would be far-reaching and complicated, affecting not just the economy but also the very fabric of society.

Deregulation evolved into more than just an economic policy; it turned into a philosophy, shaping how people thought about governance and public welfare. At its core was a key question: what role should the government play in people's lives? Supporters of deregulation pushed for less oversight, insisting that the market was not just a place for business but also a space for personal freedom and creativity. On the other hand, critics raised valid concerns, questioning the wisdom of letting markets run wild without any checks, cautioning that the most vulnerable might suffer the most in a system without safeguards.

As public conversations shifted, the debates around deregulation took on deeper meanings. They highlighted important societal values, showcasing the tension between the desire for economic freedom and the need to ensure fairness and equity. It became a clash of ideas, balancing individualism with collective responsibility—a conflict that would fuel discussions for years to come.

Amid these economic and ideological pressures, deregulation emerged as a compelling force, a rallying point for those advocating for less government involvement. The vision of a liberated market captivated many, leading them to believe that prosperity was just waiting to be unlocked by cutting bureaucratic red tape. However, history would later reveal that while deregulation could indeed spur growth, it could also expose hidden vulnerabilities that had been carefully managed under strict regulations.

The legacy of this period is intricate, weaving together stories of both success and challenges. As deregulation gained momentum, it sparked discussions that would resonate for generations. From financial markets to environmental regulations, the outcomes of these changes would impact individuals and communities alike. The effects of this transformative time continue to shape our world today, inviting us to think critically about the balance between freedom and responsibility, autonomy and accountability.

As we explore the complexities of deregulation and its consequences, we come to understand that grasping the economic context and motivations behind this movement is crucial. This insight not only sheds light on the past but also provides valuable lessons for the future. It encourages us to reflect on how we define the roles of government and the market in shaping our shared future, while acknowledging the ongoing relationship between regulation and deregulation that continues to define our economic landscape. The experiences from this historical moment serve as both a cautionary tale and a source of guidance, reminding us of the importance of thoughtful discussion and careful analysis as we navigate the challenges of an ever-changing world.

Pivotal Legislative Changes

In the late 20th century, the United States saw a dramatic shift in its economic landscape, primarily due to significant legislative changes that redefined how the government interacted with various industries. The push for deregulation stemmed from a mix of economic struggles, changing ideas, and a strong belief in market-driven solutions. As lawmakers aimed to free different sectors from previous regulatory restrictions, a series of landmark laws emerged, each promising to boost competition, lower prices, and give consumers more choices. However, while these legislative changes aimed to spark economic growth, the results turned out to be much more complicated.

One of the key moments in this wave of deregulation was the Airline Deregulation Act of 1978. This landmark legislation sought to lift the airline industry from the heavy hand of government control. Before this act, the federal government tightly regulated routes, ticket prices, and who could enter the market. This created an environment that stifled competition and innovation. The 1978 law aimed to remove these controls, allowing airlines to set their own prices and choose their routes based on what consumers wanted. Supporters celebrated it as a win for consumer freedom, imagining a world where travelers would benefit from greater competition and lower fares.

Initially, the Airline Deregulation Act produced amazing changes. Airlines thrived, new carriers sprang up, and the number of available routes grew rapidly. Ticket prices dropped, and travelers found themselves with more options than ever before. But this new freedom also brought along a number of unexpected challenges. The airline industry soon faced instability, with ticket prices and service quality fluctuating wildly. Companies focused on profits often led to aggressive cost-cutting, which hurt working conditions for employees and resulted in a decline in customer service. The competitive environment created a two-tier system, where savvy travelers could navigate the shifting fares to find great deals, while many others struggled with unpredictable pricing and varying service levels.

While the airline industry was going through these ups and downs, the financial sector was set for its own shake-up with the Gramm-Leach-Bliley Act of 1999. This legislation removed long-standing walls between commercial banks, investment banks, and insurance companies, significantly changing the landscape of American finance. Supporters claimed that this move would lead to exciting innovation, allowing financial institutions to provide a wider range of products and services and increase competition.

After the Gramm-Leach-Bliley Act passed, the financial industry did see a surge in mergers and diversification. Previously separate financial services came together, creating mega-banks that could offer consumers all-in-one packages. However, this newfound freedom also opened the door to serious instability. The risks tied to combining various financial activities became painfully obvious during the 2008 financial crisis, when the mixing of banking, investing, and insurance exposed systemic weaknesses. The lack of proper regulatory oversight contributed to a reckless environment where complex financial products spread unchecked. Ultimately, the very institutions that were supposed to provide stability found themselves at the center of chaos, leading to widespread economic turmoil and forcing a reevaluation of the assumptions behind deregulation.

Deregulation didn't stop with airlines and finance; it also made waves in telecommunications. The Telecommunications Act of 1996 marked a crucial turning point for this industry. This law aimed to encourage competition and break the monopolistic hold of traditional phone companies, allowing new players to enter the market and giving consumers a flood of choices. For a while, it seemed like deregulation had delivered on its promises, as people enjoyed lower prices and more options.

However, as time passed, the reality proved to be more complex. While consumers initially benefited from reduced prices and expanded choices, the long-term effects of the Telecommunications Act raised concerns. A few dominant companies began to emerge, raising questions about market concentration and the true extent of competition. What started as a promise of more choices evolved into a situation where a small number of corporations wielded significant power over the industry, leading to a paradox where, despite more options, the market began to echo the monopolistic tendencies that deregulation aimed to dismantle.

The Energy Policy Act of 2005 showcased the complexities of deregulation in yet another sector. Passed in the wake of the 2001 energy crisis, this law aimed to boost competition in the energy market while promoting alternative energy sources. By encouraging the deregulation of electricity markets, the act sought to spark investment and innovation in energy production. However, the outcomes varied significantly. While some areas benefited from increased competition, others experienced sharp price hikes and service interruptions. Relying on market forces to dictate energy supply revealed the challenges of deregulation in an industry where stability and reliability are crucial.

These examples illustrate a common theme—deregulation, often pursued for efficiency and consumer benefits, yielded mixed results that deserve careful thought. Each industry provides valuable lessons about the various impacts of these legislative changes, showing us that progress is rarely straightforward. The story of deregulation is filled with both successes and setbacks, and its legacy continues to shape discussions on the role of government in market management.

As we think about the effects of these legislative changes, it becomes clear that the goals behind deregulation often clash with the complex realities of how markets operate. The push for competition and innovation can lead to unintended issues, including problems with fairness, safety, and stability. Lawmakers face the challenging task of finding the right balance between unleashing the market's potential and ensuring that proper protections are in place to support consumers and workers. The experiences of deregulation across different sectors serve as a cautionary tale, highlighting the need for careful analysis and thoughtful discussions when creating policies that can alter the very fabric of our economy.

The lessons learned from these significant legislative changes remind us that while the promise of deregulation can be enticing, we must also be aware of the potential risks and challenges it brings. As society grapples with the complexities of a changing economic landscape, the impact of deregulation continues to spark important conversations about the need for regulation, oversight, and the careful balance between market freedom and public welfare.

Ideological Debates

At the core of the conversation about deregulation lies a clash of beliefs that goes far beyond simple policy discussions. On one side, supporters of deregulation argue that less government involvement in markets leads to greater efficiency, a boost in innovation, and more choices for consumers. Business leaders, economists, and free-market enthusiasts present these views with great passion, resonating in boardrooms and classrooms alike. They believe that when businesses are released from strict regulations, creativity can thrive, allowing them to quickly adapt to market demands and customer preferences. In their story, deregulation is the hero, freeing industries from outdated practices and creating an environment that fosters growth.

However, if we take a look at the other side of this debate, critics share a different perspective. They warn that without regulation, we risk creating monopolies, market failures, and a host of negative side effects that can have serious consequences for society. They point to events like the 2008 financial crisis and various environmental disasters that occurred due to lack of oversight as stark reminders of the dangers of letting the market run unchecked. This isn't just an academic debate; it has real impacts on the lives of millions, affecting everything from job security to environmental health.

The historical backdrop of these ideological discussions helps us understand why regulatory frameworks exist and why government intervention in markets can be necessary. The U.S. has a rich history of regulation, often shaped by the economic climate and societal values of different periods. For instance, the rise of industry in the late 19th and early 20th centuries led to significant regulatory efforts aimed at curbing corporate abuses and ensuring fair labor practices.

Fast forward to the late 20th century, and we see a shift toward deregulation, driven by a belief in the power of the free market. These ideological swings reflect broader cultural attitudes toward government, economics, and individual freedom.

Supporters of deregulation argue that, at its core, markets are best suited to distribute resources effectively. They believe that competition fuels innovation, lowers prices, and improves quality as businesses strive for consumers' attention. The thinking is that with fewer restrictions, companies can pivot quickly, responding to consumer needs in ways that a heavily regulated environment might hinder. In this view, the free market is like an ecosystem where the most efficient and innovative players rise to the top, benefiting both consumers and the economy.

Business leaders often share success stories that bolster the argument for deregulation. They highlight examples of industries that have thrived after regulations were lifted, claiming that increased investment and job creation were direct results. Advocates frequently mention the tech sector, especially the rapid growth of the internet and mobile technologies, which flourished in a less regulated environment. They argue that the quick pace of innovation in these areas showcases the potential of a deregulated market, where creativity and consumer demand are the only limits.

Economists often add their voices to this

discussion, supporting the idea that competition leads to the best results. They argue that the market is a self-correcting system. When businesses pursue their own interests, the theory suggests, they will inadvertently serve society's broader needs by providing better products and services at lower prices. This idea connects with the classic economic principle of the "invisible hand," which implies that individuals chasing their own goals also contribute to the overall good of the community.

Yet, this optimistic view of deregulation isn't without its challengers. Critics argue that unregulated markets can descend into chaos, often resulting in monopolistic behaviors that actually hurt competition. The banking industry during the 2008 financial crisis serves as a powerful warning for those who support a completely free market. The lack of regulatory oversight allowed financial institutions to engage in reckless behavior, including risky lending and creating complicated financial products that few understood. The resulting economic collapse starkly reminded us that without adequate regulations, markets can fail dramatically, leaving taxpayers to pick up the pieces.

Environmental issues are another key aspect of the debate over deregulation. Supporters of stronger regulations often point out the severe consequences that can arise when industries self-regulate. The Deepwater Horizon oil spill in 2010 stands out as a clear example, highlighting the risks of insufficient oversight in the pursuit of profit. Critics argue that the push for deregulation in the oil and gas sector created a mindset that favored quick profits over long-term safety and environmental responsibility. Events like this one raise critical questions about how to balance economic interests with ecological care.

The voices in this conversation are diverse and passionate. Policymakers struggle to create laws that find the right balance between encouraging innovation and protecting consumers and the environment. Economists sift through data to determine how deregulation truly impacts economic growth and social well-being. Consumer advocates push for more transparency and accountability, challenging practices that compromise public safety for profit. Even business leaders face tough decisions as they navigate the competing demands of growth, regulation, and ethical conduct.

As the debates over deregulation keep evolving, it's clear that there isn't a simple answer. Each industry has its own challenges and opportunities, which call for approaches tailored to their specific situations. The lessons we've learned from the past help guide us in navigating the future of deregulation. The ongoing discussions about the government's role in the market are not just theoretical; they have real-life effects on individuals and communities, impacting everything from job availability to environmental well-being.

Understanding these ideological debates is crucial for anyone wanting to grasp the complex world of deregulation. The dialogue isn't just a clash of opinions; it reflects our values, priorities, and hopes as a society. As we consider the effects of deregulation, we should weigh potential benefits against risks, striving for a balanced approach that promotes innovation while ensuring public safety.

Ultimately, the journey toward a deeper understanding of deregulation shows us that we need to remain watchful and flexible. The challenges posed by deregulation call for careful discussion, as different stakeholders work through the ever-changing realities of the market. The debates will surely continue, driven by the dynamic shifts in our economy and society. As we think back on the ideological battles that have shaped our regulatory landscape, we should keep an open mind, learning from both past successes and failures to pave the way forward that respects both innovation and responsibility.

CHAPTER 2: TRANSFORMATIONS IN AIR TRAVEL

Opening the Skies

In the mid-20th century, the skies weren't just seen as symbols of freedom; they were more like a heavily guarded fortress. Strict rules determined which airlines could fly, the routes they could take, and how much they could charge for a ticket. This meant that air travel offered limited choices, high prices, and a tight grip on the market by just a few airlines. Travelers could only dream of hopping on a plane without having to navigate significant hurdles put in place by these regulations. But everything changed in 1978 with the Airline Deregulation Act, which kicked off a whirlwind of changes that would completely transform the airline industry and the way millions of people traveled.

The Airline Deregulation Act was a game-changer for air travel in the United States. Gone were the days when the government dictated which airline flew to which city and at what price. This new law removed the strict price controls and route limitations that had been in place since the dawn of commercial aviation. Suddenly, airlines could enter and exit markets freely, leading to fierce competition that brought prices down and made flying accessible to many more people than ever before.

Before the act, it was a bit like playing a boring game of Monopoly where only a few players had the power and rules were rigid. After the act, the game changed entirely. Picture everyone scrambling to create new routes and services. Southwest Airlines is a perfect example of this entrepreneurial spirit. Founded in 1967, it began with a focus on a niche market in Texas but quickly took advantage of deregulation. By offering short flights and skipping unnecessary extras, Southwest created budget-friendly travel options that resonated with price-conscious travelers. Word spread about their low fares and straightforward approach, and soon, people were flocking to them, sparking a transformation in how we think about flying.

This transformation didn't just help one airline; it sent shockwaves throughout the industry. Other airlines found themselves needing to rethink their pricing and business models to keep up. JetBlue, which started in 1998, became another shining example of this new era. With fun marketing and a focus on customer service, JetBlue introduced the idea of "high-value" flying—offering affordable fares while still providing decent service. Travelers were finally able to enjoy perks like in-flight entertainment and free snacks without breaking the bank. This fresh approach forced older airlines to adapt or risk losing their passengers to these agile newcomers.

The impact of deregulation didn't stop at the major airports. Regions that had felt isolated began to experience newfound connections. Small towns and underserved areas were suddenly on the radar of airlines eager to tap into these newly opened routes. Cities like Roanoke, Virginia, and Key West, Florida, saw a boom in travel options as airlines jumped at the chance to meet the demand for accessible flying. What once took hours by car or a long train ride now turned into a quick flight on a regional jet, creating new opportunities for tourism, business, and personal connections.

The social changes were significant. With air travel becoming more affordable, it allowed people from all walks of life to take trips that had once seemed out of reach. Families finally had the chance to visit distant relatives, and college students could pursue internships or jobs far from home. Flying transformed from a luxury experience to a common way for everyday Americans to get around. More than just moving from one place to another, travel became a way to grow personally and connect with others.

Additionally, this new competitive environment changed how consumers approached travel. Travelers became savvier, using emerging travel websites and fare comparison tools to their advantage. It was no longer just about taking the first fare they found; people could search for the best deals and figure out the complexities of airline schedules with just a few clicks. This shift empowered consumers, giving them more influence in a marketplace filled with options.

But it wasn't all smooth sailing. As airlines rushed into new markets, the initial excitement over low fares was met with concerns about service quality and reliability. In the race for market share, many carriers cut costs, sometimes at the expense of safety protocols. These shortcuts led to some incidents that raised red flags about aviation safety standards. While deregulation brought in competition and new ideas, it also highlighted the challenges and potential risks of a less regulated environment.

Reflecting on the legacy of the Airline Deregulation Act reveals a complex story. It opened the skies and made air travel available to many more people, encouraging exploration and connection that changed both the economy and society. Yet, it also serves as a reminder of what can happen when competition takes precedence over oversight, reminding us all of the fine line between making air travel accessible and ensuring safety.

The rise of new airlines is paralleled by the stories of routes that disappeared when carriers pulled out of less profitable markets. Air travel, once a luxury for the few, became a common way for people to get around. However, this newfound accessibility has sparked ongoing debates about its cost. As we think about the effects of deregulation, it's important to recognize how our choices have shaped the skies we travel today.

Looking back at how the airline industry evolved after deregulation, it's clear that these changes impacted not just prices and access but the very spirit of travel. The ability to book a flight on a whim, the excitement of discovering new places, and the connections made along the way are all gifts of the legislative changes that opened the skies. This transformation brought valuable lessons—lessons that still resonate in our ongoing conversations about regulation, competition, and safety in the aviation world. Moving forward, we must find a careful balance to ensure the benefits of deregulation do not come at an unacceptable cost to safety and consumer trust.

Safety and Competition Challenges

The newfound freedom in the skies brought about by deregulation came with its own share of bumps along the way. Air travel became cheaper and easier to access, but beneath the surface, another struggle was brewing—a struggle over safety in the aviation industry. Transitioning from a tightly controlled system to one that welcomed competition led to unexpected outcomes. With rising stakes, airlines felt the pressure to provide lower fares and innovative services. But a pressing question hung in the air: at what cost to safety?

Deregulation allowed airlines to operate without the old restrictions, sparking a rush of new airlines jumping into the market as they chased what consumers wanted. However, this new atmosphere was driven by more than just a desire to serve passengers better or offer more routes; it was fundamentally about profits. The chase for profit quickly eclipsed the crucial need for strict safety standards. Cost-cutting measures began to surface, threatening the very safety protocols that had once been reliable. This time marked a growing conflict between running efficiently and upholding the principles meant to protect the flying public.

One heartbreaking illustration of this conflict occurred with the tragic crash of Alaska Airlines Flight 261 in 2000. The MD-83 plane, on its way from Puerto Vallarta, Mexico, to San Francisco, suffered a catastrophic failure in its horizontal stabilizer, resulting in a loss of control and a crash into the Pacific Ocean. Tragically, all 88 passengers and crew members on board lost their lives. Investigations uncovered that the airline was aware of ongoing issues with the aircraft's mechanical systems but chose to delay necessary repairs due to financial concerns. The push to cut maintenance costs amid fierce competition resulted in compromises that placed safety on the back burner, with executives weighing profit margins against the urgent need for proper aircraft maintenance.

In the wake of the disaster, the National Transportation Safety Board (NTSB) conducted a comprehensive investigation, revealing a history of the airline not effectively addressing maintenance problems. The NTSB's findings pointed to a culture that favored cost savings over safety. The aftermath of the crash prompted a reevaluation of regulations, leading to closer scrutiny of airline maintenance practices and a call for stronger oversight to prevent similar incidents. While the immediate response included a renewed commitment to safety protocols, it also uncovered an uncomfortable reality: competition could undermine even the best-intentioned safety measures.

The Alaska Airlines incident was not the only tragic event that highlighted the safety challenges tied to deregulation. Similar pressures were seen in other serious accidents that shook the industry. For example, the crash of Air Midwest Flight 5481 in 2003, which resulted in the deaths of 21 passengers, served as another sobering reminder of the risks posed by a deregulated environment. The Beech 1900D aircraft faced serious mechanical issues during takeoff, leading to a fatal stall. Investigations showed that the airline had overlooked essential maintenance tasks, a decision driven in part by the competitive pressures to keep costs down and maximize profits.

In light of these tragedies, regulatory agencies struggled to adapt to the rapidly changing landscape of the aviation industry. The Federal Aviation Administration (FAA) recognized that traditional oversight methods were falling short in the competitive climate brought about by deregulation. Consequently, the agency sought to implement stricter safety protocols, urging airlines to prioritize safety over profit. However, these regulatory efforts often met resistance from the industry, which argued that tighter regulations could hinder their ability to innovate and serve their customers effectively.

The ongoing tug-of-war between competition and safety was apparent in how the industry responded to regulatory changes. Airlines, eager to maintain their profit margins in a cutthroat marketplace, frequently argued that increased oversight would restrict their operations and innovation. This reliance on cost-cutting measures, aimed at lowering ticket prices, raised a crucial question: could airlines stay profitable while ensuring the safety of their passengers?

In response to these pressures, some airlines attempted to boost safety through enhanced training programs and updated maintenance protocols. Yet, the effectiveness of these initiatives often remained overshadowed by the reality that many airlines still struggled to balance the competing demands of profitability and safety. The culture of cost-cutting persisted in some operations, as companies prioritized financial health over the integrity of safety measures.

The narrative surrounding deregulation and its impact on airline safety is complex and highlights the difficulties of balancing competition with responsible oversight. As the industry evolved, it became clear that the effects of deregulation were widespread, influencing everything from operational standards to how consumers viewed safety. Passengers began to question whether the push for lower fares had unintentionally compromised the safety they assumed was guaranteed when boarding a plane.

Case studies of major accidents spurred broader discussions about the responsibilities of airlines in a competitive market. The inherent tension between profit and safety prompted a reevaluation of the industry's structure and regulations. Regulatory agencies began to realize that consumer trust in air travel relied not just on affordability but also on the assurance that safety was a top priority.

As this new focus on safety emerged, airlines found themselves under greater scrutiny. Customers became more discerning, often asking for transparency regarding maintenance records and safety procedures. The call for accountability rang throughout the industry as travelers sought assurance that their well-being was a priority. Airline executives faced the challenging task of navigating a competitive landscape while also being held responsible for their safety records.

The dialogue surrounding safety and competition gained urgency amid increasing public awareness and calls for regulatory reform. As the aviation industry faced turbulence from public outcry and regulatory changes, it became clear that the landscape was shifting. The challenge now was to find a way forward that ensured the benefits of deregulation didn't come at the expense of passenger safety.

Amid this complex situation, one important takeaway became clear: the safety of air travel is a shared responsibility that goes beyond regulatory agencies and airlines. The collective awareness of consumers plays a vital role in shaping industry practices. As passengers grew more informed about the implications of deregulation, they began exercising their power as consumers, making choices based on safety records and operational practices. The competitive nature of the airline industry sparked a change in consumer behavior, as travelers increasingly sought to balance affordability with safety.

The ongoing discussion about safety resonates throughout the airline industry. A stronger emphasis on safety doesn't have to stifle competition; instead, it can serve as a spark for innovation and improvement. Airlines that recognize the value of prioritizing safety will likely build greater consumer trust and loyalty, creating a competitive edge that goes beyond just pricing.

In the wake of notable accidents and increased scrutiny, airlines found a chance to redefine their commitment to safety. Companies began to understand that investing in safety protocols, transparent practices, and employee training could bring long-term advantages that outweighed the short-term benefits of cost-cutting. Those that embraced this mindset not only improved their operational standards but also developed a reputation for excellence in safety, a crucial asset in an industry characterized by fierce competition.

As the aviation industry continues to change, it finds itself at a crossroads where lessons from the past can illuminate the path ahead. The challenges posed by deregulation have unveiled the complexities of ensuring safety in a competitive environment, prompting a fresh look at practices that may have previously been overlooked. Striking a balance between accessibility and safety will require cooperation among airlines, regulators, and consumers.

The push for a safer aviation environment reflects the resilience of the industry. By reflecting on past mistakes and adapting, airlines can move forward with the understanding that safety is not just a necessary operation but a fundamental promise between carriers and passengers. It's a commitment that goes beyond pricing strategies —a promise to ensure that every journey prioritizes the well-being of everyone on board.

As we look back on the ongoing evolution of the airline industry in the wake of deregulation, the importance of safety remains clear. The lessons from past tragedies remind us that staying vigilant in upholding safety standards must never falter, even in a highly competitive environment. By placing passenger safety first, airlines can continue to build a future where the skies are not only open but also safe for everyone who takes to the air.

Market Dominance

The airline industry has seen a dramatic change since the days of deregulation. As airlines competed fiercely for market share, mergers and acquisitions began to reshape the landscape. This drive for profits often resulted in the concentration of power among a few major airlines, transforming the way we experience air travel. Today, just a handful of dominant carriers have emerged from this whirlwind of mergers, fundamentally changing not only the competitive scene but also the flying experience for countless travelers.

Mergers have played a critical role in this transformation. Notable unions, like that of

United Airlines and Continental Airlines, along with the American Airlines and US Airways merger, stand out as pivotal moments that reshaped the airline world. These significant changes were often justified by promises of better efficiency, improved services, and a larger market presence. But a closer look at economic principles surrounding monopolies and oligopolies reveals a more complicated picture.

When we talk about these mergers, we can think about them in terms of economic theory. A monopoly means one company has total control over the market, while an oligopoly involves a few companies holding a large amount of power. The consolidation we see in the airline industry has created an oligopoly where a small number of airlines significantly influence prices and services. This situation raises some important questions: What does this mean for the choices available to consumers? How does less competition affect prices and the quality of service? And ultimately, what does it mean for everyday flyers?

Airlines often claim that mergers will lead to cost savings. Supporters argue that when companies join forces, they can cut down on wasteful practices and offer better services, resulting in lower fares for consumers. However, history shows that this ideal is not always the reality. Instead of seeing cheaper prices, many travelers end up with fewer options and sometimes even higher costs. For example, after

United and Continental merged, many popular routes had fewer available flights, allowing the new company to control pricing with little competition to challenge them. Passengers who once enjoyed many flight options suddenly found themselves limited, with a handful of airlines dictating the terms.

A similar story unfolded after the American-US Airways merger. Once this merger was completed, travelers quickly noticed a drop in the number of affordable fares on certain routes. This shift rippled through the market, as the newly combined airline adjusted its pricing strategies to take advantage of its dominant position. For those used to the price competition between airlines, the change was a shock. Suddenly, flying became less about finding good deals and more about managing expenses.

But the effects of reduced competition go beyond just ticket prices. When there are fewer choices, service quality can suffer as well. In a near-monopoly or oligopoly environment, airlines may not feel the pressure to keep high service standards. After all, if passengers have limited options, airlines might not prioritize customer satisfaction as much. As we've seen in recent years, the flying experience often shifts from meeting customer needs to focusing solely on operational efficiency.

For instance, issues like flight cancellations, lost luggage, and poor customer service have reached new heights. With fewer airlines competing for passengers, the motivation for airlines to maintain quality has weakened. Consumers find themselves stuck in a situation where their concerns may go unheard, leading to both financial and emotional stress.

Given these challenges, the role of government regulation becomes crucial. Ensuring that the airline industry operates fairly and transparently is vital. Yet, many feel the current regulatory framework is lacking, struggling to keep up with the fast-paced changes driven by mergers and acquisitions. Antitrust laws are particularly important for understanding how the industry is regulated. Many legal experts argue for stronger enforcement of these laws to address the issues that arise from market consolidation.

Policymakers share these concerns, worried about the long-term effects of such dominance in the airline sector. The balance of power has shifted dramatically, favoring a few key airlines, raising questions about the future of competition. Regulators must face the challenge of finding ways to protect consumer interests in an environment where the incentives have changed.

As we look ahead to the airline industry's future, the relationship between deregulation and market dominance becomes even clearer. New technology and changing passenger behaviors are set to shape the industry in exciting but challenging ways. For instance, digital platforms now allow travelers to easily compare prices and services, which can enhance competition and transparency, even in a market dominated by just a few players.

However, there's also the risk of further consolidation looming on the horizon. With ongoing economic pressures on airlines, the urge to merge may continue. The future of the airline industry may rely on finding the right balance between promoting competition and ensuring safety and quality of service. As consumer preferences evolve, the call for transparency and ethical practices will likely grow. How well airlines respond to these expectations may be key to their success moving forward.

The implications of market dominance in the airline industry are significant and layered. The concentration of power among a few airlines changes not just pricing and service quality, but the entire experience of flying. As the industry continues to evolve, the need to ensure fair competition and protect consumers must stay front and center in discussions among regulators, industry players, and travelers.

With the complex interplay of economic interests, regulatory hurdles, and changing consumer demands, the future of the airline industry remains uncertain. What is clear is that we must stay alert to protect the interests of travelers. The lessons learned from past mistakes, marked by declines in service and regulatory gaps, should guide today's decisions and influence the industry's future.

As we navigate this landscape of mergers, acquisitions, and market dominance, the voices of consumers must not be overlooked. The direction of the industry will be shaped not only by corporate strategies but also by the rising expectations of passengers. Providing affordable, high-quality air travel should be at the heart of the airline industry's mission—a mission that balances the need for profits with the commitment to prioritize the experiences and safety of those who choose to fly.

In these times of rapid change in the airline industry, the responsibility of managing these complexities falls on everyone involved. With a focus on innovation, responsiveness, and accountability, the industry can redefine itself in ways that benefit not just the airlines, but more importantly, the passengers who depend on their services. As competition heats up in the skies, ensuring consumers get a fair deal will be a cornerstone of a healthy and thriving airline industry.

CHAPTER 3: SHIFTING LANDSCAPES IN TELECOMMUNICATIONS

Disruption of Monopolies

The telecommunications world we know today is a far cry from what dominated the late 20th century. There was a time when just a few giant companies controlled the airwaves and cables that linked people all over the globe. It's almost hard to picture a period when one company had so much say over how and when we communicated. But that was the reality for many consumers in the United States and beyond until a mix of technological, political, and social changes sparked a major shift toward competition and deregulation.

This story traces back to the founding of

the American Telephone and Telegraph Company (AT&T) in the 1880s. Initially, it aimed to enhance communication, but over time, it transformed into a massive entity that dominated the telecommunications market by the mid-20th century. AT&T didn't just offer telephone service; it controlled the very infrastructure needed for these services, giving it incredible power over pricing, service quality, and access. Unfortunately, this kind of control stifled innovation and limited options for consumers. Like many monopolies, the needs of the people took a backseat to the interests of the company.

The government's response to AT&T's monopolistic practices was a crucial turning point for the industry. The breaking point came in the 1970s when dissatisfaction grew among lawmakers, consumer advocates, and budding entrepreneurs who realized the limitations of having one all-powerful player in the field. After years of legal wrangling and regulatory examination, the U.S. Department of Justice reached a landmark settlement in 1982 that broke AT&T into seven regional companies, often called the "Baby Bells." This pivotal moment marked the beginning of a new chapter, paving the way for competition in a sector that had been long dominated by a single entity.

With AT&T's breakup, the telecommunications industry suddenly found itself bursting with competition. Regional carriers like Bell Atlantic and Southwestern Bell could now operate independently, creating an environment where innovation thrived. Smaller providers began to enter the market, many focusing on niche services or specific geographic areas. These new players brought fresh ideas and technological advancements, fundamentally changing the way we communicate.

This wave of competition set the stage for rapid growth in telecommunications technologies in the following decades. The advent of cellular technology, for example, benefited significantly from this shift. With many carriers striving to attract consumers, companies started to invest heavily in research and development to stand out. The outcome was an explosion of mobile services and devices that have become essential in our daily lives. Gone were the days of heavy rotary phones attached to a wall; they were replaced by sleek smartphones that allow not just voice calls, but also internet browsing, gaming, and much more—all at the tap of a finger.

However, while breaking up monopolies sparked innovation, it also introduced challenges we still face today. One pressing concern that arose from this new competitive environment was the risk of uneven service quality. As multiple carriers rushed to enter the market, many focused on rapid growth instead of ensuring consistent coverage. This led to disparities in service availability, especially in rural and underprivileged urban areas. The digital divide became apparent, highlighting the stark reality that while some consumers enjoyed state-of-the-art technology and services, others found themselves left behind, unable to connect in our increasingly digital world.

The struggle to maintain service quality amid fierce competition became a key issue after deregulation. In their quest to draw in customers, companies often slashed costs, sometimes jeopardizing service reliability. A catchy ad for a low-priced plan might entice someone to switch providers, but the allure of cheaper rates could hide bigger problems like network congestion, poor customer service, and delayed repairs. While customers appreciated lower prices and more choices, they also had to navigate a market that, at times, seemed more concerned with competition than meeting the basic needs of its users.

This situation brings up an important question: how do we make sure that the benefits of deregulation and competition don't come at the expense of service quality and fairness? Balancing innovation with consumer welfare remains a tricky challenge for regulators and policymakers. As we look ahead in this changing landscape, it's crucial to reflect on the lessons learned from past disruptions and to apply that wisdom as we tackle current and future issues.

As we navigate an era of rapid technological growth, we may need to rethink how we approach regulation and oversight. The lines between telecommunications and internet technologies are increasingly blurred. The rise of Over-The-Top (OTT) services like Netflix, WhatsApp, and Skype has added another layer of complexity to the telecommunications scene. These platforms have taken advantage of the infrastructure provided by telecom companies, leading to a scenario where traditional providers must compete not only with one another but also with a multitude of internet-based services that often operate outside the typical regulations.

Deregulation has changed the game and sparked an ongoing conversation about the future of telecommunications and the role of government in shaping that future. As consumers grow used to immediate access to information and smooth communication, service providers feel the pressure to keep up with changing expectations. The challenge lies not just in the technology itself, but also in addressing the lingering gaps in access and service quality.

As we work through these challenges, we must be cautious of the downsides of deregulation. While it's important to celebrate the innovations that have come from increased competition, we should also remember that a truly fair telecommunications landscape can't rely solely on market forces. A strong regulatory framework, informed by a clear understanding of the unique complexities of this industry, is essential to ensure that the benefits of deregulation reach everyone, not just those who can afford it.

As we stand on the brink of new advancements in telecommunications, the experiences of the past remind us that progress isn't always straightforward. Each disruption presents both opportunities and hurdles, and finding the right balance between fostering competition and ensuring that society remains connected is vital. In a world where connectivity increasingly shapes social, economic, and political engagement, how we regulate telecommunications will undoubtedly influence the future we aim to build. The pressing question is how to navigate this exciting new landscape while keeping equity, quality, and innovation at the forefront of our minds.

Technological Accelerations

The world of modern telecommunications is an exciting mix of new ideas, swift changes, and fierce competition. At the center of this vibrant shift is deregulation, which has acted like a rocket booster for technology and has brought us into an era where staying connected is easier than ever. When regulations started to fade away, they didn't just open the door for new businesses; they sparked a rush of technological advancements that transformed how we communicate and interact with one another.

Take mobile communication, for instance.

It's a shining example of the creativity that deregulation has unleashed in the telecommunications field. Remember the early days of cell phones? Back then, they looked more like heavy bricks than the sleek devices we carry today. Those initial clunky models were primarily used as a lifeline for busy people, but they've evolved into powerful smartphones that can do just about anything—from video chatting and online shopping to controlling our smart homes. This incredible transformation didn't happen overnight; it resulted from teamwork among telecommunications companies, tech innovators, and regulators, all working together to stretch the limits of what we can achieve.

When restrictions were lifted, it created a ripe environment for competition. Telecommunications companies no longer had to stick to old service models; they could innovate, try new ideas, and yes, even face setbacks. Each effort brought them closer to the next big breakthrough. Companies poured resources into research and development, eager to outshine each other in winning over consumers. This friendly competition led to rapid advancements in mobile technologies, highlighted by the rollout of 3G, 4G, and now the push for 5G networks.

The launch of 4G technology was a game changer. With speeds that allowed for high-definition video streaming and smooth social media access, it completely changed the way we enjoy content. No more frustrating buffering—users could stream movies and music effortlessly, just by swiping a finger. The smartphone morphed into more than a communication tool; it became our go-to device for entertainment, learning, and getting things done. Suddenly, everything we could possibly want was right at our fingertips, available anywhere and anytime, reshaping how we behave and connect with one another.

As we move into the 5G era, the excitement is palpable. Promising even faster speeds and the capability to connect numerous devices at once, 5G networks are gearing up to launch us into the world of the Internet of Things (IoT). Just imagine a future where your fridge orders groceries automatically, your car communicates with traffic lights to find the best route, and smart cities manage energy use efficiently—all thanks to the advanced connectivity brought about by these new technologies. The possibilities seem limitless, and as these innovations unfold, they will redefine our daily lives, work environments, and how we connect with each other.

However, the journey toward this interconnected future isn't without its bumps. While many cities enjoy strong mobile connectivity, rural areas still struggle to access the latest technologies. The digital divide is a pressing issue, showing the gaps that remain in this fast-moving landscape. Many rural residents grapple with limited access to high-speed internet and dependable mobile services, which puts them at a disadvantage in a world that's increasingly reliant on technology. In an age where tech is crucial for education, jobs, and healthcare, this divide could limit opportunities for many individuals.

Telecommunications companies and regulators need to realize that just because technology is advancing doesn't mean everyone has access to it. It's crucial to ensure that underserved areas aren't left behind as innovation races forward. Initiatives that aim to expand broadband infrastructure and make it more affordable are essential for closing this gap. Policymakers have a key role to play in encouraging investment in rural connectivity, creating an environment where all communities can succeed.

In addition to mobile technology, the rise of broadband internet has also changed how we communicate. With the barriers removed, the landscape for high-speed internet access has grown dramatically. Internet service providers emerged and began competing with each other to offer faster and more reliable services. This competition led to innovations, but it also raised important questions about service quality and affordability.

For businesses, widespread access to broadband has been a revolutionary change. Companies can now connect with customers and clients instantly, breaking through geographic barriers. E-commerce has blossomed, enabling small businesses to flourish by reaching a global audience. The traditional brick-and-mortar model has evolved into a vibrant and varied business scene, where both startups and established firms harness the power of the internet to grow and engage with customers.

Education has also been transformed by advances in broadband technology. With high-speed internet, students can tap into a wealth of information and learning resources from almost anywhere. Online learning platforms have democratized education, allowing people from all walks of life to pursue opportunities that may have previously been out of reach. This shift in technology has opened up a world of lifelong learning, giving individuals the skills and knowledge they need to thrive in a constantly changing job market.

Looking at the success stories of companies that have thrived in this space, it's clear that deregulation has set the stage for groundbreaking solutions that meet the needs of our interconnected society. Take Netflix, for example. It changed how we consume media by using broadband connectivity to offer streaming services. By shaking up traditional entertainment models, Netflix not only altered our viewing habits but also pushed the entire film and television industry to adapt and innovate.

Likewise, tech startups have jumped on

the opportunities that a deregulated environment provides. With the freedom to utilize mobile and internet technologies, these companies are making strides in various sectors. From telehealth solutions that let patients consult with doctors from home to financial apps that give us access to services at our fingertips, the innovations that have come from deregulation are wide-ranging and impactful.

As we think about the transformative effects of these technological accelerations, it's evident that deregulation has played a crucial role in driving societal progress. The merging of mobile communication and broadband access has reshaped our lives, changing how we connect, work, and interact with each other. Yet, with these rapid changes, we also need to stay aware of the challenges they bring.

There's a clear need for solid regulatory frameworks. As competition continues to grow and new technologies emerge, we must make sure the benefits of deregulation reach everyone, especially those who might get left behind. Policymakers should find a careful balance that encourages innovation while also protecting consumer interests and promoting fair access.

Ultimately, the story of technological acceleration in telecommunications is one of immense potential mixed with the need for inclusivity. The pursuit of progress should never overshadow the importance of ensuring that everyone can join in this digital revolution. As we look ahead to a future filled with rapid changes, our collective challenge will be to guarantee that the amazing technologies emerging from deregulation serve everyone, creating a world where connectivity is a right, not a privilege. Through teamwork, creativity, and smart policies, we can create a future where technology acts as a bridge, not a barrier, bringing us together on a shared path to a brighter tomorrow.

Addressing Inequalities

The growth of telecommunications has been an exciting journey, but it comes with an undeniable reality that we can't ignore: the digital divide. Even with all the advances in technology and communication, there are still big gaps in access to these tools. The digital divide represents the inequality in how available and usable technology is, especially when it comes to internet access. This divide shows a serious split in our society, separating those who are online from those who aren't, often based on where they live, how much money they make, and their race.

Just think about the difference between urban and rural areas. In cities, where the buzz of technology is often at its peak, people can enjoy high-speed internet and the latest mobile devices. Meanwhile, rural communities struggle with slow internet or, in some cases, no access at all. It's like we've built a smooth highway for some while leaving others to travel on rough, unpaved paths.

This stark contrast raises important questions about fairness and the effects of deregulation in telecommunications.

When we look closer at deregulation, we see that while it has brought more competition and innovation, it has also made existing inequalities worse. Big telecom companies tend to invest in crowded urban areas where they can make more money. As a result, rural communities are left with limited choices and poor service. This isn't just an issue of convenience; it affects access to education, job opportunities, and essential services. When internet access isn't spread out fairly, the benefits of the digital age aren't shared equally.

The problem goes beyond just infrastructure; it also involves affordability and digital know-how. For many low-income families, internet access can be too expensive, creating a tough cycle. Students without reliable internet struggle to complete assignments and connect with educational content online. Adults may find it hard to apply for jobs or even secure employment without basic internet access. So, the digital divide acts as a barrier, making it harder for people to improve their lives and move forward.

To tackle these inequalities, we need to take a well-rounded approach. Several policies have emerged to address the digital divide and boost access in underserved areas. One notable example is the Federal Communications Commission's (FCC) Lifeline program, which offers discounted phone and internet services to low-income households. This program has helped many families get connected, but it has faced criticism regarding how well it works and how many people it reaches.

The Lifeline program serves as a reminder that good intentions don't always lead to effective solutions. While it aims to help, many eligible families either don't know about it or find the application process confusing. On top of that, some service providers may hesitate to join the program, which limits its overall effectiveness. This highlights the need for programs to not only have good goals but also to be easy to use and understand.

The challenge of improving infrastructure also plays a key role. Expanding broadband access to rural areas often requires a lot of money, which can discourage telecommunications companies from investing in these less populated markets. To tackle this, various government initiatives have worked to encourage investment in rural broadband infrastructure. Grants and subsidies can offer the financial support needed for companies to expand their services to areas that are often overlooked.

Nonprofit organizations have also stepped up to help close the digital divide. Many have launched programs that focus on digital literacy, providing training to help individuals navigate the online world effectively. Teaching basic computer skills and internet usage can empower communities, allowing them to fully embrace the benefits of technology. Bridging this gap requires not just access but also the skills to use these tools effectively.

There are plenty of success stories that show it is possible to make progress in closing the digital divide. For example, community-driven broadband initiatives have popped up across the country. In some rural areas, local governments and community groups have joined forces to create their own broadband networks, bypassing the limitations of larger providers. These grassroots efforts highlight the power of working together and show how communities are dedicated to ensuring their members have access to the digital world.

A shining example is the small town of Ammon, Idaho. City officials recognized that residents were struggling with poor internet service, so they took action. They worked hard to develop a municipal fiber-optic network that would benefit everyone. This effort led to a high-speed internet network that not only provided reliable service but also attracted businesses and boosted economic growth. Ammon's story demonstrates how local efforts can yield incredible results when communities unite to advocate for their needs.

In addition to local networks, various tech companies are starting to invest in projects that aim to improve connectivity. Companies like Microsoft and Google have launched initiatives focused on rural areas, providing solutions like satellite internet and wireless technology. These efforts from the private sector are crucial, as they not only tackle the issue of access but also emphasize the importance of teamwork between public and private organizations in narrowing the digital divide.

Another important aspect of addressing inequalities is promoting digital literacy in communities. Programs that teach residents how to use online platforms and access digital resources can lead to significant change. Public libraries, for instance, have become centers for digital education, offering workshops and resources for community members. By improving digital skills, individuals can engage more effectively in the digital economy, enhancing their job prospects and overall quality of life.

As we think about the digital divide, it's also important to consider the impact of emerging technologies like artificial intelligence and automation. These innovations have the potential to change industries and job markets, but they also risk widening the gap if certain groups are left behind. Policymakers need to address these challenges head-on, making sure that everyone has the chance to engage with and benefit from new technologies.

Equity in technology means more than just

having internet access. It includes the ability to use technology for personal and professional growth, to engage with digital platforms in meaningful ways, and to thrive in a connected world. Because of this, we must focus on inclusive policies that support not only connectivity but also education and empowerment.

As we look ahead, the lessons learned from working on the digital divide can shape how we approach future technological advancements. Ensuring that everyone, no matter their background or location, can join the digital revolution will take ongoing dedication from policymakers, businesses, and community organizations. Bridging the digital divide isn't just an act of kindness; it's an investment in our future together.

The efforts to reduce gaps in access to telecommunications highlight a basic truth: technology should connect us, not divide us. As we continue to innovate and grow our digital landscape, we must stay alert to ensure everyone can enjoy its benefits. The journey toward fairness in telecommunications is not only possible but essential. By fostering an inclusive environment where technology is accessible to all, we can harness its power to uplift communities, improve lives, and drive progress for generations to come. By doing this, we can change the story surrounding the digital divide from one of exclusion to one of opportunity, where technology serves as a bridge that brings us together instead of a barrier that keeps us apart.

CHAPTER 4: FINANCIAL SECTOR'S NEW FRONTIERS

Global Banking Opportunities

The world of finance is like a vast ocean that is always changing. Over the last few decades, it has gone through major shifts, mainly driven by changes in regulations. Banking, once limited by strict national rules, has opened up to a global stage. This isn't just a historical note; it's a complete change in how financial institutions function and connect across countries.

To really understand the opportunities that exist in global banking today, we first need to look back at the history of banking regulations. For much of the 20th century, banks operated under tight rules aimed at keeping things stable and protecting customers. These rules were designed to control the flow of money, limit risky behavior, and create fairness among financial institutions.

However, as we reached the late 20th century, many voices began calling for fewer restrictions. They believed that relaxing these rules would encourage competition, spark innovation, and ultimately create a more efficient financial system.

The impact of this push for less regulation was significant. The 1980s and 1990s saw a loosening of regulatory controls. Banks started to engage in activities that had previously been seen as too risky. Mergers and acquisitions became the norm as financial institutions aimed to grow both at home and abroad. This change led to an environment where banks could experience remarkable growth, creativity, and—most importantly—competition.

Emerging markets, which were often ignored in earlier decades of financial regulation, became hotspots for banks eager to tap into new opportunities. Countries in Asia, Africa, and Latin America were no longer viewed merely as sources of resources; they became exciting markets with great potential for rapid growth. The rigid boundaries that once defined where banks could operate were broken down, and financial institutions started to think globally. They recognized the huge potential in economies that were evolving quickly.

With this new global mindset came innovative financial products. Structured financial instruments, derivatives, and asset-backed securities emerged, providing banks with tools to diversify their investments and manage risks. While these products allowed banks to enhance their operations, they also brought more complexity and potential dangers. For example, while financial derivatives promised higher returns, their complicated nature often concealed the risks involved.

As banks explored these new territories, the landscape of international banking changed dramatically. The interconnectedness of the global economy meant that events in one part of the world could have far-reaching effects elsewhere. Banks began to build relationships with foreign partners, open branches in new markets, and adapt to different regulatory environments. This flexibility became key for banks aiming to succeed globally.

However, while there were many opportunities, the era of deregulation also brought challenges. With fewer rules, the pressure to make profits grew. Institutions that used to prioritize caution began chasing higher returns, sometimes at the expense of sound practices. The 2008 financial crisis serves as a stark reminder of what can happen when innovation outstrips regulation. As banks took on riskier behaviors, the very stability of the financial system was put in jeopardy.

The lessons learned from that turbulent time have led to a reassessment of the guiding principles for global banking. Following the crisis, there has been a call for a balanced approach to deregulation—one that encourages new ideas while making sure that systemic risks are kept in check. Policymakers are starting to see that a stable financial system relies not just on reduced oversight but also on transparency and accountability.

Finding this balance is crucial as banks venture into new areas. With the rise of digital currencies, fintech companies, and decentralized finance, traditional banking is being reshaped. It's vital for regulators to stay on top of these changes. Emerging technologies can revolutionize finance by making transactions quicker, cheaper, and more secure. Yet, these innovations also carry risks that shouldn't be overlooked.

Through all these opportunities and challenges, one thing is clear: banking is going through a period of change. The global market is more connected than ever, and the way financial transactions happen is always evolving. Banks that adapt to these shifts while focusing on ethical practices and protecting consumers will be in the best position to thrive in the future.

As we explore the effects of deregulation further, it's important to remember that the opportunities in global banking go beyond just numbers on a spreadsheet. They reflect the relationships built between banks and their customers, the trust established in communities, and the potential for economic growth that can benefit entire countries.

In navigating this dynamic landscape, financial institutions need to find a balance between taking advantage of opportunities and managing risks, ensuring that their drive for innovation doesn't compromise stability. As the banking sector looks ahead, it stands at the brink of significant transformation, ready to harness the benefits of globalization while remaining mindful of past lessons. The path forward will demand not just a vision but a commitment to responsible practices that protect the financial well-being of both institutions and individuals alike.

Heightened Risks

In the vast world of finance, what often appears sophisticated can sometimes be incredibly complicated. Over the last few decades, we've seen a remarkable rise in complex financial tools. These include everything from derivatives to mortgage-backed securities and collateralized debt obligations, all of which are now staples of the financial markets. They're designed to help manage risks, generate capital, and improve liquidity, but they also create a breeding ground for confusion, especially when there's little regulatory oversight.

Let's take a closer look at these complex instruments. Derivatives are contracts that derive their value from the performance of something else—like an asset, an index, or an interest rate. They can be used to hedge against risks or to gamble on future price changes. Imagine them as financial chameleons, adapting to market conditions. For example, options give the holder the right, but not the obligation, to buy or sell an asset at a set price, while futures contracts require parties to buy or sell an asset at a predetermined price on a specific date. While these tools can be powerful when used wisely, they can lead to severe losses if not fully understood or if misused.

Mortgage-backed securities (MBS) and collateralized debt obligations (CDOs) add even more layers of complexity. MBS are created by pooling various mortgages and selling them as bonds to investors, providing a steady income from mortgage payments. However, when the economy takes a hit, the risks tied to these securities can be devastating, as seen during the 2008 financial crisis. CDOs bundle different types of debt, including MBS, into sections called tranches that offer varying levels of risk and return. The complicated nature of CDOs makes it hard for investors to truly grasp what they are buying, leading to widespread mispricing and risk management issues.

The rapid growth of these financial products often coincides with a lack of regulatory oversight. Financial institutions frequently played a risky game of hide-and-seek with their responsibilities, crafting new products faster than regulators could catch up. When banks heavily leveraged MBS and CDOs, the protective measures designed to keep the financial system stable began to wear thin. This made it tough for institutions to accurately gauge their risks, resulting in catastrophic outcomes when the situation turned sour.

As these instruments became more complex, so did the nature of systemic risks. Systemic risk is the chance that a significant disruption in the financial system could impact the overall economy. This risk is especially concerning in deregulated settings, where the close ties among global financial institutions can lead to a chain reaction of failures. The 2008 financial crisis is a stark reminder of this. When Lehman Brothers collapsed, it sent shockwaves through the financial sector. The interconnectedness of institutions meant that the failure of one could jeopardize the stability of many others, highlighting just how fragile the system was without proper oversight.

While interconnectedness can enhance liquidity and share information across borders, it also poses risks. If one institution falters, it can create a ripple effect, spreading financial trouble rapidly. When banks are linked through complex products, it becomes incredibly difficult for regulators to keep tabs on the associated risks. The idea of "too big to fail" became a very real concern, showing the urgent need for regulations that could address these systemic weaknesses.

One major factor driving risk-taking

behavior in financial institutions has been the lure of quick profits. Deregulation fostered a culture where immediate gains often overshadowed the importance of long-term stability. This was further amplified by performance-based pay models. Executives and traders, motivated by bonuses tied to short-term results, felt encouraged to chase aggressive strategies without fully considering the risks. Consequently, many institutions opted for quick profits over sustainable practices, leading to reckless decision-making.

This trend toward high-risk behavior is evident in the stories of financial institutions that faced significant consequences due to their risky approaches. Lehman Brothers is perhaps the most infamous example. Their rapid expansion into mortgage-backed securities and CDOs, without sufficient risk management, set the stage for their dramatic collapse in 2008. The fallout from this event rippled throughout the global economy, underscoring the interconnectedness of the financial world.

Bear Stearns provides another cautionary tale. Known for heavy investments in mortgage-related assets, it was one of the first significant casualties of the financial crisis. A loss of confidence from creditors led to a liquidity crisis, which ultimately forced its sale to JPMorgan Chase at a fraction of its original value. The swift decline of Bear Stearns demonstrated how quickly fortunes can change for even the most secure institutions when they face rising risks and inadequate regulatory measures.

These stories illustrate the devastating outcomes that can result from unchecked risk-taking in a deregulated environment. The lessons learned are critical, indicating that if we don't adopt thoughtful regulatory approaches, we may be doomed to repeat the mistakes of the past. As the financial sector continues to evolve, it raises important questions about how we can balance innovation with regulation. With new financial technologies and products emerging, regulators must find ways to adapt quickly to manage the complexities and risks these innovations introduce.

The landscape of regulation is filled with challenges, especially as financial institutions keep innovating and changing. Current regulatory frameworks often fall short when it comes to addressing the unique issues posed by complex financial instruments. Regulators face the daunting task of staying on top of an ever-evolving industry while also protecting the financial system from potential disasters. The response to the 2008 crisis was a step in the right direction, but as we enter a new era of finance marked by technology and globalization, the lessons of the past remain relevant.

To navigate these increased risks, we need regulatory approaches that do more than just check boxes. A proactive approach is necessary —one that anticipates new risks instead of just responding to past failures. Regulators should encourage collaboration between financial institutions and oversight bodies, promoting transparency and accountability in decision-making. Only then can the financial sector build a strong framework that supports innovation while also ensuring stability.

The financial landscape keeps changing, offering both new opportunities and new challenges. The complexity of financial instruments, the nature of systemic risks, and the behaviors of financial institutions all contribute to an environment filled with heightened risks. As we think about the lessons from history, it's clear that a balanced approach is vital. We need a new regulatory mindset that takes into account the interconnectedness of global finance, the intricacies of modern instruments, and the incentives that drive institutions. As we watch innovative financial products and technologies continue to emerge, it's crucial for both regulators and institutions to stay alert, ensuring the hard lessons of the past aren't forgotten and that the financial system remains robust against future crises.

Crisis Reflections

The 2008 financial crisis is a significant chapter in economic history, filled with stories of deregulation, unchecked ambition, and complicated financial products. Its impact stretched far beyond Wall Street, shaking economies around the world. This crisis reminds us of how fragile the balance is between creativity in finance and the necessary oversight that keeps it in check. To grasp the full weight of this crisis, we need to look closely at what led up to it and think about the consequences that followed.

Before the crisis, the chase for profits was relentless, and many financial institutions took reckless risks. In the years leading up to 2008, banks, encouraged by fewer regulations, eagerly jumped into high-risk financial products. The idea of being "too big to fail" became a common belief among top executives, who stretched the limits of financial creativity to create what seemed like endless wealth. During this time, many banks operated as if they were untouchable, convinced that the government would always step in to rescue them if things went south. It was a perfect storm fueled by greed, innovation, and a lack of accountability.

At the center of this financial whirlwind was the housing market. The American Dream of owning a home was aggressively pushed, and banks eagerly handed out mortgages to anyone who applied—often without proper checks. The rise of subprime mortgages highlighted a bigger issue: a financial system that had lost its sense of caution. Both lenders and borrowers were swept up in the thrill of easy credit, leading to a surge in home purchases and skyrocketing housing prices. But beneath this shiny surface, problems were brewing, and the housing bubble was about to burst.

As homeowners began to default on their mortgages, the complex network of financial products started to come apart. Mortgage-backed securities and collateralized debt obligations, which were once seen as smart financial solutions, quickly turned into ticking time bombs. The assets that were meant to reduce risk instead became the triggers for widespread failure. When mortgage defaults surged, the value of these securities plummeted, sending shockwaves through the markets. Banks found themselves burdened with massive amounts of toxic assets, and trust in the whole system started to fade.

The fallout was devastating. Lehman Brothers, once a giant in investment banking, collapsed under the weight of its unsustainable practices and filed for bankruptcy in September 2008. This shocking event froze credit markets and sent the global economy spiraling into chaos. The interconnectedness of financial institutions, once thought to be a strength, turned into a web of vulnerability. Banks that seemed solid one day found themselves on the edge of failure the next, leading to unprecedented bailouts and government interventions.

As the crisis unfolded, it became painfully clear that a lack of regulatory oversight had created a perfect setup for disaster. Institutions that had once been seen as sturdy pillars of stability were exposed as fragile and vulnerable. The crisis revealed a fundamental truth: without checks and balances, catastrophic outcomes can arise. In the wake of this turmoil, there was a widespread reevaluation of regulatory frameworks, leading to major reforms aimed at preventing a similar disaster from happening again.

In response to the crisis, the Dodd-Frank Wall Street Reform and Consumer Protection Act was introduced to address the systemic failures that had been revealed. The main aim was to increase transparency and reduce risks within the financial system. A key feature of Dodd-Frank was the creation of the Volcker Rule, designed to limit banks from engaging in proprietary trading. This rule was meant to curb the reckless behavior that had run rampant in the financial sector before the crisis. The goal was to ensure that banks would focus on serving their customers instead of chasing short-term profits.

While the intentions behind these reforms were admirable, putting them into practice was not without its challenges. Critics pointed out that some regulations were overly complicated and stifled innovation. Financial institutions found themselves wading through a maze of compliance requirements that often seemed to hinder progress rather than promote it. Striking the right balance between encouraging growth and ensuring stability became a hot topic, with ongoing discussions about how effective the reforms really were.

The lessons from the 2008 financial crisis continue to resonate today as we talk about deregulation and oversight. With new financial products and technologies emerging all the time, the memories of past mistakes loom large. We find ourselves at a crucial point, trying to balance the need for innovation with the necessity of regulation. It's a tightrope walk that requires careful attention to avoid falling into the traps that led to the crisis in the first place.

As we see the rise of cryptocurrencies and fintech innovations today, the need for a balanced regulatory approach is even more urgent. The fast-changing financial landscape calls for regulators to be flexible and quick to respond. Finding the right balance is key to creating an environment where innovation can flourish while also protecting against potential risks.

Looking back, we must recognize that the financial sector is always changing. The connections between institutions, the complexity of new products, and the global nature of finance mean that risks can come from unexpected places. A strong regulatory framework should not only learn from past failures but also prepare for future challenges. Policymakers need to encourage cooperation between financial institutions and regulators, promoting transparency and accountability in decision-making.

In this light, the 2008 crisis serves as a powerful reminder of the consequences that can arise from ignoring the fragile balance between innovation and oversight. It highlights the need for constant vigilance, proactive measures, and a readiness to adapt as the financial world evolves. This crisis was not just a temporary setback; it was a turning point that reshaped our understanding of finance, regulation, and how they work together.

As we look toward the future of the financial sector, we must carry the lessons learned from the past with us. The quest for profit should never overshadow the basic principles of sound risk management and ethical responsibility. We are standing on the brink of a new era in finance, filled with the promise of incredible advancements, but also shadowed by the mistakes of the past. The real challenge is to create a regulatory environment that embraces innovation while ensuring the stability of the financial system—a balance that needs ongoing care and thoughtful consideration.

Ultimately, moving forward means committing to learning from history, grasping the nuances of risk, and fostering a culture that supports ethical behavior and sustainable practices. The 2008 financial crisis starkly illustrated what can happen when the financial world operates without adequate oversight. As we reflect on past crises, we should also look ahead with determination, working to build a financial system that meets society's needs while remaining strong against future challenges. In doing this, we can honor the lessons learned and strive for a more stable and fair financial future.

CHAPTER 5: ENERGY MARKET DYNAMICS

Competitive Hopes vs. Reality

In the world of energy markets, the idea of deregulation sparked a wave of excitement, much like the thrill of a child on Christmas morning. Supporters of deregulation were quick to sing its praises, imagining a future where consumers would enjoy the benefits of competition, complete with lower energy prices and a variety of innovative services. This vision was appealing to many, painting a picture of lively markets where competition would effortlessly balance supply and demand, making energy flow as freely as ideas in Silicon Valley.

Deregulation advocates argued passionately that government control stifled creativity and held back competition. They envisioned a bright new future where market forces would determine prices, inspiring investment and leading to groundbreaking technology advancements. The promise was enticing: if consumers could choose their energy providers, companies would have to innovate to keep up or risk falling behind. They believed this competition would not only improve services but also save households money.

To grasp this wave of enthusiasm, we should look back at the groundwork laid in the early 1990s, especially in states like California and Texas. California's attempt at deregulation was touted as a shining example of what could be achieved. The state aimed to create a competitive marketplace for electricity, giving consumers the power to pick their own providers. The allure of lower prices and increased choices spread hope across the public. Similarly, Texas implemented a deregulated electricity market, aiming to create competition that would benefit consumers while encouraging innovation among service providers.

However, as the saying goes, good intentions can lead to unintended consequences. The lofty expectations set by these ambitious policies soon met the harsh realities of the market. The statistics that once supported the idea of lower costs and increased competition began to unravel. In California, energy prices didn't just decrease; they skyrocketed. As companies rushed to take advantage of the new freedom, the system quickly became overloaded.

What started as an ideal vision of a competitive energy market soon turned into a battleground where the interests of consumers and providers clashed, and the outcomes were stark. The promise of lower prices faded as market manipulation surfaced. Companies exploited loopholes and engaged in practices that caused prices to spike unexpectedly, leaving consumers in shock. The well-known California energy crisis, marked by rolling blackouts and skyrocketing costs, shattered the belief that deregulation could fix all the energy sector's problems.

Adding to the complexity, consumer behavior in these deregulated markets often didn't match expectations. In theory, empowered consumers would seek out providers offering the best deals, driving prices down through competition. However, studies showed a different reality; many consumers felt overwhelmed by the complicated world of energy pricing. Faced with a dizzying array of choices, they often opted for the easiest route, choosing familiarity over better options.

Surveys indicated that a large number of consumers didn't switch providers, mainly because they didn't understand the intricacies of energy tariffs and how the market worked. This lack of action effectively stifled the competitive pressure that deregulation was supposed to create. Instead of selecting providers based on price and service quality, many settled for what they knew, which kept them tied to higher costs and poorer service.

The economic principles behind these

observations reflect the realities of consumer choice and market competition. For competition to work effectively, consumers need to be informed and actively engaged in the market. However, this ideal often crumbles under the weight of consumer apathy and the complexity of choices. The promises of a deregulated market began to feel hollow as evidence grew that, instead of empowering consumers, the new landscape had turned into a confusing maze that left many feeling lost and disappointed.

Furthermore, it became clear that regulatory bodies, intended to protect consumers, often lost power and influence in this new setup. The reduced oversight that came with deregulation meant there were fewer tools available to address price spikes and shield vulnerable populations. As energy prices surged, especially in places like California, it was evident that the lack of a safety net left many consumers exposed and at risk.

All of these realities paint a complicated picture, where the initial excitement for a competitive marketplace became entangled with the messy realities of the market. The lessons learned from California and Texas provide important insights into the effects of deregulation. As we sift through the aftermath of these experiences, it becomes clear that while the idea of a consumer-driven energy market was appealing, its execution faced challenges that many had not foreseen.

Through careful examination of historical data and case studies, it's apparent that deregulation did not produce the universally positive results that its supporters had promised. The expectations were high, but the outcomes fell short. Price spikes, service disruptions, and a disengaged consumer base were just a few of the consequences that arose from the unchecked enthusiasm for deregulation.

The initial excitement surrounding deregulation reminds us that market interventions are not one-size-fits-all solutions. The ideal vision of competition can quickly become an illusion, especially when faced with the complexities of human behavior and market dynamics. For consumers, this has meant navigating a landscape that is often more confusing than empowering, where the promise of choice comes with the reality of unpredictability.

Ultimately, the story of energy market deregulation is one of contradictions—a mix of hope and disappointment that reflects larger themes in the deregulation debate. While the early enthusiasm was understandable, the unfolding realities reveal a more intricate narrative, one where the gap between expectation and reality continues to grow. The lessons learned from these experiences urge us to rethink the stories we tell about deregulation, encouraging a deeper understanding of what true competition means in the complex world of energy markets.

Manipulation and Crisis

The California energy crisis of the early 2000s serves as a powerful reminder of how good intentions can spiral into disaster when there's not enough regulatory oversight. The idea of deregulation sounded enticing, drawing in both consumers and policymakers with the promise of a marketplace where competition would thrive. Unfortunately, what actually happened was far from the bright vision initially painted. Instead of a smooth transition, the situation quickly turned chaotic, revealing how some used the very system meant to protect consumers for their own gain.

At the center of this crisis was a deregulation plan designed to create a competitive environment where energy providers would compete for consumers' business. The goal was simple: lower prices and better service for everyone. In theory, this should have worked out perfectly—an energy paradise filled with innovation and efficiency. However, as we've seen time and time again, things can go wrong when the foundation isn't strong. In this case, the weak points in the plan gave profit-driven market players a chance to take advantage.

To understand what happened during the California energy crisis, we first need to look at the deregulation framework set up in the state in the late 1990s. California's leaders had big dreams of reshaping the energy sector, giving consumers the freedom to choose their electricity providers. While it sounded promising, the reality fell far short of the optimistic words that accompanied the changes. Rather than a lively, competitive market, the outcome was a breeding ground for exploitation and deception.

As soon as the energy market was deregulated, it caught the eye of both established companies and new players eager to make a quick buck. Enron, in particular, became the poster child for the unethical practices that defined this crisis. The company's leaders quickly spotted the regulatory loopholes, using their insider knowledge to create artificial shortages. This was not just a case of a few bad apples; it was a coordinated effort to exploit a weak system for profit.

Enron, along with other companies, started manipulating supply and demand to create a false sense of scarcity. They developed trading strategies that involved withholding energy during peak demand times, which pushed prices to shocking levels. In their hands, the energy market transformed into a playground for trickery instead of a fair competition that benefited consumers. Meanwhile, everyday people were left scratching their heads as their utility bills climbed, even on sunny days in California.

The underhanded tactics of these energy traders didn't stop at just manipulating supply. Companies employed various schemes, like making false claims about how much electricity was available and shutting down power plants for "maintenance" just when everyone needed energy the most. These deceptive actions made it look like there was a real crisis, leading to rolling blackouts and a wave of public anger. California's once-bright energy future dimmed as citizens faced not only unexpected power outages but also skyrocketing energy costs.

As the crisis deepened, it became clear that consumers weren't the only ones suffering. Public outrage hit a boiling point, prompting intense political pressure on regulatory agencies to step in. California's Governor Gray Davis found himself under fire, leading him to make tough decisions to bring some order back to the chaos. Ultimately, the state legislature stepped in, reversing some of the deregulation changes and reinstating oversight in hopes of stabilizing the energy market.

But by that point, the damage was already done. The California energy crisis changed how the public viewed both the energy market and the regulators in charge. Many consumers came away feeling let down by a system that had promised them choice and competition, but instead left them vulnerable to exploitation. The idea of a deregulated market became a cautionary tale, highlighting the dangers of not having enough oversight in an industry that is crucial to daily life.

Looking back, this crisis teaches us about the risks of deregulation when oversight is weak.

While supporters may argue that deregulation can spur innovation and lower costs, the experience in California shows how easily market dynamics can be distorted. The long-term fallout reached beyond just financial losses; it shook the public's trust in regulatory institutions and sparked a more cautious view of market forces.

In the years after the crisis, California had to face the reality that deregulation, without proper checks and balances, could lead to serious disruptions in essential services. Consumers started to realize that true competition needed more than just letting companies run wild. They recognized the vital role of regulatory frameworks in protecting public interests and ensuring that market players couldn't exploit vulnerabilities for their gain.

The California energy crisis didn't happen in a vacuum; it's part of a broader story about deregulation and market dynamics. The lessons learned from this turbulent time have significant implications for energy policy and regulation, not just in California but across the nation and beyond. In the wake of the crisis, many policymakers began reassessing their approaches to deregulation, aiming to strike a balance between promoting competition and safeguarding consumers.

For many, the energy crisis served as a wake-up call—a realization that the initial excitement surrounding deregulation was built on shaky foundations. Policymakers and regulators have since worked to develop a stronger framework, incorporating lessons from California into their strategies for governing energy markets. This renewed focus has sparked discussions on how to create effective regulations that can keep pace with the evolving energy landscape while protecting consumers from manipulation.

Yet, challenges still linger. The energy market is constantly changing, with new technologies and renewable energy sources adding complexity to regulatory efforts. The threat of manipulation remains a real concern, reminding us that staying alert is crucial when dealing with these complexities. Striking the right balance between encouraging innovation and ensuring market fairness is a tricky task, and the California energy crisis stands as a powerful reminder of what can happen when that balance is off.

The aftermath of the crisis also impacted public trust significantly, as many consumers began questioning the motives of both energy companies and regulatory bodies. This loss of confidence created ripples that influenced energy policy discussions for years. Citizens began demanding transparency and accountability, understanding that they deserved a fair and reliable energy market rather than one plagued by manipulation.

As we continue to navigate the challenges

posed by energy markets, it's crucial to keep the lessons from the California energy crisis at the forefront of our minds. Policymakers, industry leaders, and consumers all need to stay involved, pushing for a system that prioritizes fairness, sustainability, and oversight. By embracing a cooperative approach that reflects on past experiences, we can better understand the complexities and risks associated with the energy landscape.

Ultimately, the California energy crisis is a powerful reminder of the fine line between innovation and exploitation. While deregulation holds the potential for lower costs and greater competition, it also carries the risk of manipulation and market distortions without proper oversight. As we look ahead to the future of energy policy, one thing is clear: we must aim for a framework that encourages real competition while protecting consumers from the dangers of a deregulated market.

Security Concerns

As we explore the complexities of deregulation in the energy sector, it's impossible to ignore the security issues that arise when markets operate with less oversight. While the excitement of deregulation can be tempting, it can also make consumers vulnerable to risks that could impact not just their finances, but their daily lives. The thrill of lower prices and more choices can swiftly turn into fear when the systems designed to support these markets start to falter.

To grasp the heart of these security challenges, we need to look at how deregulation has changed the reliability of our energy grids. Energy isn't just a product; it's what keeps our lives running smoothly. It lights up our homes, powers our businesses, and drives our economy. When the balance of supply and demand gets out of whack, the results can be severe. The decentralized approach of deregulated markets often creates weaknesses that can be exploited by bad actors or lead to significant problems during natural disasters.

Recent events show just how delicate this balance can be. Take the Texas power crisis in February 2021 as a prime example. A polar vortex brought freezing temperatures to the state, creating chaos. The deregulated energy grid, which was supposed to thrive on competition, found itself in deep trouble. The Electric Reliability Council of Texas (ERCOT), which manages the state's electric grid, quickly became overwhelmed. Many power plants were not equipped to handle winter weather, resulting in widespread failures just when electricity was needed the most. Rolling blackouts left millions in darkness, and for many, this wasn't just a nuisance; it was a critical situation.

How did we end up in such a risky scenario? The principle behind deregulation pushes for a free-market approach that often values profit over preparation. Companies, in their quest for customers, can cut corners to save money. While this might bring quick financial rewards, it weakens the long-term reliability of our energy systems. Experts have pointed out that the lack of strict regulations in Texas led to insufficient investment in necessary infrastructure improvements. In an industry where severe weather can lead to disasters, being unprepared is a recipe for trouble.

Looking at California's past energy crisis reinforces the ongoing debate about deregulation and its effect on market stability. Just like in Texas, California's crisis was marked by weak regulatory oversight, allowing profit-driven companies to take advantage of system flaws. It raises a significant question: when left unchecked, can competition genuinely build a reliable energy market, or does it simply lead to chaos?

Cybersecurity is another critical area of concern. As energy systems become more interconnected and rely heavily on digital technology, the threat of cyber-attacks becomes increasingly significant. Bad actors could disrupt energy supplies, causing chaos in people's lives and livelihoods. The infamous Colonial Pipeline ransomware attack in 2021, which resulted in fuel shortages across the Eastern United States, serves as a stark reminder of how vulnerable our critical infrastructure is. Energy grids are now prime targets for hackers, and the potential damage could be catastrophic.

A survey by the U.S. Department of Energy found that nearly one-third of energy companies reported experiencing some form of cyber-attack. This trend is troubling, especially since many companies in deregulated markets may prioritize profits over investing in security. The fragmented nature of these markets makes it even harder to implement effective security measures, leaving consumers exposed to serious risks.

When talking about energy security, we can't forget about consumer protection. The allure of deregulated markets often hides the fact that not all consumers benefit equally. While some enjoy the perks of competition, others may feel left out. Differences in access and service quality can emerge as companies focus on the most profitable customers. The promise of choice can feel empty when some consumers find themselves at the mercy of a market that favors those with deeper pockets.

For example, a family living in a rural area may struggle to find competitive rates because fewer providers want to serve less populated regions. Consequently, the dream of lower energy costs isn't shared by everyone. Those who are most at risk—low-income families, the elderly, and rural residents—often bear the brunt of a deregulated system that doesn't adequately safeguard their needs.

This brings us to the crucial role

of regulatory bodies. Although the idea behind deregulation is to minimize government intervention, it's evident that some level of oversight is necessary to ensure market stability and protect consumers. Regulatory agencies can act as the guardians of public interest, making sure energy markets operate fairly and equitably. But when deregulation leads to less oversight, as we've seen in various energy crises, the consequences can be devastating.

Regulatory agencies need to adapt to the realities of a changing energy landscape. With the rise of renewable energy sources and decentralized power generation, regulators face the tough task of protecting consumers while promoting innovation. The future of energy policy must find the right balance between encouraging competition and ensuring consumers are not left vulnerable.

So, how do we create a safer and more reliable energy market? Policymakers, energy providers, and regulators must join forces to develop strong strategies that focus on consumer protection while also fostering market innovation. This involves investing in infrastructure, prioritizing cybersecurity, and ensuring that regulatory frameworks can adapt to the fast-evolving energy landscape.

Emerging technologies, like smart grids and energy storage, present exciting opportunities to improve grid reliability. These innovations can help reduce risks from extreme weather and cyber threats. However, putting them into practice needs careful regulation to prevent market abuse. In a deregulated environment, the temptation for companies to cut corners could jeopardize the reliability of these new technologies if not closely monitored.

As we think about the long-term impacts of deregulation on energy market security, it's clear that the stakes are high. A functioning energy market is crucial for the health of our economy and the well-being of our communities. Finding the right balance between competition and oversight isn't just an academic issue; it's vital for the future of our society.

The energy market landscape is rapidly changing, with new technologies and renewable sources reshaping our ideas about production and consumption. However, these changes also bring challenges that need our attention. The experiences of California and Texas serve as powerful reminders of the need for regulatory oversight to protect the public interest. As we look ahead, it's important to learn from past mistakes and work towards a system that safeguards consumers while promoting innovation.

We need to keep a close eye on the dynamics of deregulated markets and their potential impacts on energy security. By taking a proactive approach to regulation, all stakeholders can collaborate to build a more resilient energy future—one that protects consumers and ensures reliable power for everyone. The lessons from past crises shouldn't just be historical notes; they should guide us as we navigate the challenges of deregulation in the energy sector. The future of our energy infrastructure is at stake, and we must act thoughtfully and decisively.

CHAPTER 6: RESHAPING THE TRUCKING INDUSTRY

Opening Roads to Competition

The trucking industry has gone through some huge changes over the years, all shaped by rules that once tightly controlled it but eventually opened the door to competition. To really understand how we got here, let's take a step back to the early 20th century, when the trucking industry was just getting started. Before the Motor Carrier Act of 1980, the industry was tangled up in a maze of regulations meant to keep things orderly but, ironically, they stifled both innovation and competition.

In the 1930s, the Interstate Commerce Commission (ICC) set up the rules for the trucking industry. The goal was straightforward: protect the interests of established carriers, ensure stable pricing, and prevent wild competition that could spiral into damaging price wars. But these rules created a situation that felt more like a monopoly than a real market. With tight price controls and restrictions on where companies could operate, it was nearly impossible for new businesses to join the scene. If someone wanted to start a trucking company, they had to jump through numerous hoops, proving there was a need for their service and getting permission from the ICC. This system limited the number of carriers, allowing a few dominant players to control the market, often leading to a lack of motivation to innovate.

During this time, trucking saw little in the way of progress. Companies had no real reason to improve services or invest in new technology since they were guaranteed a protected market. Customers had no choice but to deal with whatever the established firms offered, which often wasn't focused on keeping them happy. Looking back, it's clear that the trucking industry was only operating at a fraction of what it could achieve, held back by rules that stifled competition and creativity.

As the economy changed and the need for efficient logistics grew, the weaknesses of this regulated system became painfully obvious. Business leaders and policymakers began to question whether such strict regulations were truly effective. They argued that if competition increased, prices would go down, service would improve, and everyone would benefit. This idea gained traction throughout the 1970s, eventually leading to the groundbreaking decision to deregulate the industry.

The Motor Carrier Act of 1980 was a game-changer. It lifted many of the previous restrictions on trucking companies, allowing them to operate more freely and encouraging new businesses to enter the market. This act wasn't just about removing rules; it fundamentally changed how the trucking industry worked. The results were immediate and dramatic. The number of trucking companies exploded, jumping from just a handful of major players to thousands of new carriers that appeared almost overnight.

Numbers from the years after deregulation tell a fascinating story. The amount of licensed trucking companies rose from about 18,000 in 1980 to over 60,000 by the mid-1990s. This surge in competition sparked innovation as companies competed for market share. Trucking firms began to offer a wider range of services, from speedy shipping to specialized hauling, addressing specific customer needs and preferences. With this newfound freedom, trucking companies could play around with pricing structures, service options, and delivery times, ultimately giving consumers more choices than ever.

One standout example of a company that thrived after deregulation is Schneider National, founded in 1935. Once the Motor Carrier Act took effect, Schneider quickly adapted, expanding its fleet and services. By focusing on operational efficiency and customer satisfaction, they became one of the largest and most respected transportation and logistics companies in the United States. Success stories like Schneider's highlight how deregulation can revitalize an industry that was once held back by red tape.

However, the flood of new competitors brought its own set of challenges. As more companies entered the market, a troubling trend emerged: the race to offer the lowest prices. While competition typically drives prices down, the relentless push for lower costs can sometimes lead to poor service quality. Smaller or less established firms often struggled to keep up standards while trying to compete on price. This raises a critical question: have the benefits of increased competition really outweighed the downsides?

With the shift to a free-market system, new regulatory challenges also popped up. The industry began facing issues related to safety and environmental standards. As the number of trucks on the road grew, so did concerns about public safety and infrastructure. Truck accidents became a significant issue, prompting some to call for the return of certain regulations to ensure companies prioritize safety and compliance. Balancing competition with public safety has become a hot topic among all those involved.

As we look at how the trucking industry has evolved, we find ourselves at a crucial point between competition and regulation. The deregulation of trucking was indeed a groundbreaking move, revitalizing an industry once stifled by excessive oversight. But while we celebrate the improvements in competition and efficiency, we must also recognize the challenges that have emerged along the way. The landscape is a lively mix of innovation, opportunity, and responsibility, continuously shaping the future of logistics and supply chain management in ways we're still beginning to grasp.

As we ponder these changes, it's clear that the journey toward competitive excellence in the trucking industry is far from over. In the pursuit of efficiency and market leadership, it's vital to keep an eye on the well-being of everyone involved in this complex system, ensuring that the drive for profits doesn't overshadow the essential values of safety, quality, and accountability. Next, we'll explore the impressive efficiency gains that have come from deregulation, looking at how technology and streamlined processes have truly reshaped the logistics landscape.

Efficiency Gains

The trucking industry perfectly illustrates the saying that necessity is the mother of invention. When the Motor Carrier Act of 1980 opened up competition, it sparked a wave of changes that transformed logistics forever. With fewer regulations holding them back, companies started to explore ways to be more efficient that had once seemed out of reach. At the heart of this shift was a drive to cut costs and improve service, all fueled by new technologies and a focus on making operations smoother.

Let's take a moment to appreciate how technology has fundamentally changed the trucking industry. After deregulation, technology became more than just an extra tool; it turned into a lifeline for trucking companies trying to navigate the new competitive landscape. For example, GPS tracking systems revolutionized how logistics were managed. No longer did truck drivers have to struggle with outdated paper maps that could lead to wrong turns and late deliveries. With GPS, planning routes became much more accurate. It's like having a personal guide that provides real-time updates on traffic, road conditions, and the fastest routes to take.

Look at a company like J.B. Hunt Transport Services, which made GPS tracking a central part of its operations. By adopting this technology, they managed to cut down on fuel use and speed up deliveries, demonstrating how smart tech investments can lead to real savings. The outcome was impressive; they achieved a 15% drop in operational costs just a few years after implementing GPS technology. This isn't just a number on a financial statement; it reflects a commitment to being leaner, quicker, and smarter in an industry where efficiency is crucial.

In addition, the rise of route optimization

software has been another major breakthrough. These programs analyze traffic patterns, weather conditions, and even driver habits to make sure every route taken is the most efficient one. It's like giving each truck a crystal ball to foresee challenges before they happen. A logistics company like C.H. Robinson, for instance, has used this kind of software to create super-efficient delivery schedules, cutting their average transit time by more than 20%. This level of efficiency doesn't just benefit the companies; it also makes customers happy—who wouldn't want their packages delivered on time?

Another significant innovation brought about by deregulation is the use of electronic logging devices (ELDs). Initially met with some pushback, these devices have proven beneficial for both drivers and companies. ELDs keep track of service hours and help ensure safety regulations are followed. But there's more to it; they provide valuable data that companies can use to improve their operations. When companies monitor driver performance, vehicle upkeep, and route efficiency using ELD data, they can make smarter decisions that enhance their bottom line.

Yet, it's not all about technology. Deregulation also led to major changes within companies, pushing many trucking firms to streamline their operations. The drive to stay competitive encouraged businesses to rethink their supply chain strategies. Lean management practices became popular in trucking, focusing on cutting waste and boosting productivity. Best practices began to emerge, showing how companies could refine their supply chains to eliminate unnecessary steps and enhance efficiency.

Take Knight Transportation, for example. They completely restructured their supply chain, using real-time data to manage inventory, maximize truck capacity, and improve delivery schedules. This approach minimized the number of empty trips—known as deadheading—and made better use of resources. By implementing these best practices, Knight Transportation not only slashed costs but also saw a remarkable 30% increase in productivity over five years. Other companies weren't just sitting back, either. As businesses aimed to outdo each other, a culture of ongoing improvement began to grow throughout the industry.

The positive impacts of these efficiency gains extend far beyond trucking companies and ripple through the broader economy. As these companies fine-tuned their operations, freight rates started to reflect these efficiencies. Before deregulation, freight rates were stable and predictable—almost as reliable as the weather forecast. However, as competition ramped up, those rates began to fall. Data from the Bureau of Transportation shows that in the decade after deregulation, average freight rates dropped by nearly 40%. This change meant lower transportation costs for businesses nationwide, giving them more room to reinvest their savings.

These lower freight rates also directly benefit consumers. Imagine this: as transportation costs shrink, businesses can offer more flexible pricing. This translates to savings on everything from our groceries to the furniture we buy for our homes. For most people, these cost reductions might go unnoticed at first, but over time, they add up. The trucking industry, in becoming more efficient, has become a cornerstone of the American economy, creating smoother supply chains that lead to better availability of goods at lower prices.

Still, this relentless quest for efficiency raises an important question: what about the environment? As companies work to cut costs, the environmental impact of their operations has become a hot topic. More trucks on the road could suggest increased emissions, and while that's a legitimate concern, the reality is more complex.

Many companies are adopting newer, cleaner technologies, and since the 1980s, the average emissions per mile have actually dropped. More firms are exploring alternative fuels and fuel-efficient vehicles as part of their sustainability efforts. For instance, UPS has invested in electric and hybrid trucks, showing that it's possible to achieve efficiency without sacrificing environmental responsibility. These advancements demonstrate that the industry is not just focused on profits but is also becoming more conscious of its carbon footprint.

Experts in the field recognize the balancing act between economic efficiency and environmental sustainability. Advocates for greener practices often call for more regulations to keep the industry accountable as it strives for efficiency. It's a tricky balance where the gains in operations must be weighed against potential environmental costs. The conversation about sustainability isn't just a side note; it's a crucial aspect of the trucking industry's future.

The changes in the trucking industry after deregulation have indeed created a more dynamic and efficient environment. Technological advancements are at the core of this evolution, helping companies maximize their capabilities and streamline their operations. The ongoing efforts to refine processes show a growing understanding of the need to adapt and innovate in a competitive market. While the economy benefits from lower prices and improved services, the discussions around environmental impact add an essential layer to this ongoing story.

The journey of the trucking industry in the years after deregulation highlights a powerful mix of competition, technology, and economic benefit. As companies navigate this landscape, the challenge remains to find a way to grow while staying accountable to the broader values of society. With every mile traveled and every delivery made, the narrative of efficiency gains in trucking continues to evolve, shaping the future of logistics in ways we are only just starting to explore.

Driver Welfare

The human story behind the trucking industry often gets lost in the chatter about efficiency, competition, and logistics. While these topics are important to understanding today's transportation landscape, they don't tell the whole story. At the center of this industry are the men and women who commit their lives to making sure that goods reach our doorsteps. The impact of deregulation—often praised for boosting efficiency—has brought significant challenges for these drivers, creating a tough and uncertain life on the road.

Let's take a moment to think about what it really means to be a truck driver in today's deregulated environment. These individuals frequently find themselves facing long hours and tight delivery deadlines, a situation made worse by the fierce competition in the industry. As trucking companies rush to meet customer demands and grab market opportunities, the pressure on drivers grows. Their working conditions can feel more like an endurance challenge than a profession, where health and safety often take a backseat to speed and efficiency.

Let's hear from some of the voices on the

road. Bill, a long-haul truck driver with over 15 years under his belt, shares what a typical week looks like for him. "It's not unusual to drive 11 hours a day, sometimes more. You're racing against the clock, and the company expects you to make those deliveries on time, no matter what." You can hear the exhaustion in his voice as he talks about missed meals, quick roadside naps, and restless nights spent in cramped truck cabs. "You start to feel like a machine, just a cog in the wheel, moving from point A to B."

When we look deeper into Bill's experience, it becomes clear that the effects of deregulation go beyond just financial worries for trucking companies. The relentless push for faster deliveries often overlooks the essential needs of drivers. Long hours on the road not only increase the risk of accidents but also take a toll on mental health. The isolation that comes with life on the road, combined with unpredictable schedules, can lead to increased stress and anxiety.

The health consequences of such demanding working conditions are alarming. Research shows that truck drivers are at a higher risk for obesity, diabetes, and heart diseases compared to other workers. A sedentary lifestyle and irregular eating habits contribute to these health risks, making the situation critical. "I've seen guys who just give up on taking care of themselves," Bill reflects, recalling friends who have succumbed to the pressures of the job. "They get so wrapped up in the numbers that they stop thinking about their health."

These deteriorating conditions aren't just personal battles; they highlight a bigger systemic issue in the trucking industry. Companies often hesitate to prioritize driver welfare, seeing it as an expense rather than an investment. In a world where every penny counts, cutting corners can seem like the easiest choice. This raises a significant question: How can the industry tackle these challenges while still staying competitive?

Job security and steady income are major concerns for drivers in this deregulated market. While there's potential for higher wages, it often comes with strings attached. Drivers face a shaky existence as demand rises and falls, leaving them vulnerable to sudden layoffs or unpredictable hours. Many drivers work as independent contractors, a setup that might sound appealing at first but often leads to exploitation. They can find themselves in a feast-or-famine situation, where a busy season brings in good pay, but during slow months, their income can drop drastically.

In this environment, wage trends have taken a sharp turn. According to the Bureau of Labor Statistics, median pay for truck drivers has stayed flat, failing to keep up with inflation. While some trucking companies have raised wages due to labor shortages, others still offer low pay, creating an uneven playing field. This uncertainty leaves many drivers wondering if their profession can provide the stability they need to support their families.

Maria, a woman who has spent the last decade driving in the southeastern United States, shares her experience. "You never know when the next paycheck will come. Sometimes I'm scrambling just to make ends meet," she says. "I love what I do, but it's hard to stay motivated when you're not sure if you'll have a job next month." Her words resonate with many drivers facing the ups and downs of the industry.

Labor unions and advocacy groups are stepping in to address these issues, recognizing that drivers need support in a market that often seems indifferent to their struggles. Organizations like the Teamsters and the United Road Transport Union are pushing for better working conditions, fair pay, and job security. Their efforts are raising awareness and encouraging discussions about the need for regulatory reform and protections for drivers.

Progress is slowly being made as lawmakers begin to understand the complexities of the trucking landscape. The Infrastructure Investment and Jobs Act, for instance, includes provisions aimed at improving truck driver safety and working conditions. However, many drivers feel like real change is moving at a snail's pace, leaving them waiting for something substantial to happen. The advocacy work being done is vital, but the pressing question remains: how do we turn these efforts into real change on the ground?

As we examine the relationship between deregulation and driver welfare, it becomes clear that a balanced approach is necessary. Encouraging competition in the trucking industry doesn't have to come at the cost of driver welfare. Insights from industry leaders suggest that finding a sustainable way forward requires cooperation among all parties involved —trucking companies, drivers, labor unions, and policymakers.

Let's take a moment to think about some of the innovative ideas that have emerged from these discussions. Some companies are trying out more flexible scheduling that puts driver well-being first while still keeping productivity in check. Others are investing in health and wellness programs to support their drivers' physical and mental health. "It's all about creating a culture where drivers feel valued," says Rick, a CEO of a mid-sized trucking firm. "If we take care of our drivers, they'll take care of our customers."

However, real change requires commitment from everyone involved. The trucking industry is at a crucial point where the balance between competition and welfare could either move it forward or hold it back. Both industry leaders and policymakers need to focus on the human side of trucking, understanding that drivers aren't just numbers on a balance sheet but vital contributors to the economy.

This complex situation shines a light on a critical part of the ongoing story surrounding deregulation. The opportunities brought about by a competitive market need to be paired with a recognition of the human factors involved. The trucking industry has the potential to flourish, but only if it prioritizes the safety, health, and welfare of those who make it all happen—the drivers.

This exploration of driver welfare serves as a small window into the broader themes related to deregulation. As the trucking industry keeps evolving, our understanding of the delicate balance between market forces and human experiences must also grow. The need for a thoughtful approach that respects workers' needs while embracing the advantages of a competitive market is more pressing than ever. The path ahead will demand open dialogue, dedicated advocacy, and a shared commitment to steering the industry toward a future that values both efficiency and the people behind the wheel.

CHAPTER 7: EVOLUTION OF CABLE TELEVISION

New Players and Platforms

In the colorful world of television, the loosening of cable industry regulations brought about a huge change, like opening floodgates that had been closed for too long. The Cable Communications Policy Act of 1984 kicked off a chain of events that transformed how we consume media forever. This law, once just a small whisper of change, now echoes in the homes of viewers everywhere as they make countless content choices. By allowing more service providers to enter the market and encouraging competition, this act made it possible for television to evolve from a handful of channels to an incredible array of options.

With these new opportunities, fresh players flooded in. As things settled down, we began to see a colorful mix of competitors reshaping the old cable TV model. Streaming services like Netflix and Hulu, which once seemed insignificant, quickly grew into major players, often overshadowing traditional cable companies. Amazon Prime Video changed the game even further by combining shopping with entertainment, offering not just shows and movies but an all-encompassing experience that merged purchasing with viewing.

These platforms didn't just show up; they brought innovative strategies that took the industry by surprise. Netflix started as a DVD rental service, but soon shifted to on-demand streaming and started investing in original shows. With hits like "House of Cards" and "Stranger Things," it didn't just join the market; it changed it entirely, pushing traditional networks to rethink their approaches. Hulu and Amazon Prime followed, each creating their own unique spaces and offerings that ramped up the competition even more.

The technological advances that came with deregulation were a huge boost for these new players. The availability of broadband internet changed everything, letting viewers access media in ways they never could before. No longer tied to a TV set and a cable cord, people could watch their favorite shows on all sorts of devices—laptops, tablets, and smartphones. Mobile viewing meant binge-watching could happen anywhere:

in coffee shops, parks, or even on the bus. This shift required not just improvements to existing technology but also new systems that could support streaming on a massive scale.

As traditional cable providers felt their grip on the market loosening, they scrambled to keep up. Some reacted with fear, while others saw new chances. Bundling services became a common strategy, with companies offering packages that included cable, internet, and phone services to keep their customers. However, this often left consumers feeling stuck with features they didn't want or need. At the same time, cutting prices became a popular tactic to attract new customers, but this could lead to unsustainable business models down the line.

For viewers, the arrival of these new competitors was a breath of fresh air. They suddenly had a wealth of choices, allowing them to decide not only what to watch but when and how. Streaming platforms served up a smorgasbord of content that catered to all kinds of tastes, from niche documentaries to blockbuster films. The excitement of on-demand viewing, along with lower subscription prices, sparked a passion among audiences eager to break free from the tight grip of traditional cable contracts.

Yet, this exciting competition brought its own challenges. The explosion of options, while thrilling, also created confusion. Viewers were bombarded with choices, making it tough to figure out which services offered the best deals for their needs. The quality of service could vary wildly from one provider to another, leaving some consumers frustrated and overwhelmed. Accessibility was also an issue; not every household had equal access to high-speed internet, which limited viewing options for many potential subscribers.

As audiences reveled in the excitement of increased competition, they also had to deal with the lingering presence of the old cable giants, who weren't going away anytime soon. Established players fought to hold onto their past while trying to thrive in this new world of deregulated television. Their strategies were diverse and often reactive, highlighting the tension between sticking with tradition and embracing innovation that defined this time.

Amidst all this competition and technological change, the true evolution of cable television took shape, illustrating the complexities of a rapidly changing market. As new platforms continued to emerge, the effects of deregulation echoed throughout the industry, challenging traditional norms and reshaping how audiences interacted with media. The rise of these new players wasn't just about who delivered content; it was also about how viewers connected with and engaged in that content, paving the way for a media landscape that was as dynamic as it was unpredictable.

As we look at this ongoing story, it becomes clear that the evolution of cable television is not just about the new players but also about the deep impact of a deregulated environment, which has forever changed our media consumption habits. With each new competitor comes a wave of possibilities, and as we prepare for what comes next, we can't help but wonder: what does the future hold for an industry still finding its way in a changing world?

Consumer Choice Dilemma

As cable television changed and competition heated up, viewers suddenly found themselves faced with a buffet of options that could rival any extravagant spread. The days of flicking through just a few channels were behind them; now, they were overwhelmed with choices. This explosion of options led to what many call the "consumer choice dilemma." The initial thrill of endless possibilities quickly became a puzzle, as having more choices didn't always mean more satisfaction.

Studies have shown that having too many options can actually cause anxiety and confusion. Picture yourself in a grocery store, standing in front of a cereal aisle packed with choices: organic, gluten-free, high-fiber, and even fun cereals shaped like cartoon characters. While it seems exciting at first, many shoppers leave the aisle feeling frustrated and unable to pick anything. This same feeling can be seen in cable TV, where viewers scroll through an endless list of channels and shows, each vying for attention. Researchers have found that as the number of options goes up, satisfaction often goes down. People can feel so overwhelmed that they struggle to make a choice, leading to what experts call decision fatigue.

We can see this in everyday life. Think about someone flipping through their cable package, only to be bombarded by a sea of channels featuring everything from niche documentaries to reality shows about competitive cake decorating. As they scroll, their interest starts to fade, and they might end up watching something entirely different or even skip TV altogether. The promise of hundreds of channels often turns into frustration instead of excitement, as viewers find it hard to connect with content that truly interests them amid all the noise.

On top of this, the rising costs of cable subscriptions add another twist to the dilemma. Even as more content options have emerged, prices have climbed. As viewers demand more from their experiences, cable companies invest in exclusive shows and high-quality programming. What used to be an affordable monthly bill now reflects the hefty price tags that come with creating must-see television. The costs have risen so much that many consumers are left wondering if it's really worth it.

It's not hard to understand the economics at play here. Producing content and securing licenses can be very pricey, especially when it comes to hiring top talent and creating engaging shows. As cable providers try to keep up with streaming services and their vast libraries, they find themselves in a costly competition. The need to lock in exclusive rights to popular shows and films translates into higher subscription fees for viewers. So, while choices may have increased, accessing those choices has become much more expensive, making consumers question if they are truly getting their money's worth.

To make matters more complicated, cable companies often bundle their services. In an effort to keep subscribers in a crowded market, they create packages that include not just cable, but also internet and phone services. While this might sound like a good deal, many viewers end up paying for channels they don't watch just to get access to the few they want. This forced bundling can create resentment, as customers feel stuck in a system that prioritizes profits over their preferences.

Recently, there has been a pushback against these bundling practices, sparking conversations about how cable television is regulated. People are calling for more transparency and choices, with some suggesting a la carte offerings that let viewers pick and pay only for the channels they truly want. However, the industry's complexities mean that significant change doesn't happen overnight, leaving many viewers frustrated and longing for a more personalized viewing experience.

As audiences navigate this maze of options and costs, a noticeable shift in viewing habits is taking place. The rise of on-demand streaming services like Netflix, Hulu, and Disney+ provides an appealing alternative to traditional cable. These platforms let users create their own content libraries, tapping into the desire for flexibility and control. The ability to binge-watch entire seasons or dive into a vast library of films at their own pace has fundamentally changed how people interact with television.

This trend of cutting the cord reflects a growing dissatisfaction with traditional cable, leading many to rethink their viewing choices. Instead of feeling swamped by countless options within a cable package, viewers can now choose platforms that suit their preferences best. The convenience of streaming, coupled with general discontent with the old model, has resulted in a steady decline in cable subscriptions as more people turn to personalized alternatives.

Looking ahead, it's interesting to consider how content delivery systems will continue to evolve. As viewers' tastes shift, the need for more customized experiences will only become stronger. The idea of a la carte options could provide a solution to the consumer choice dilemma, allowing audiences to select only the channels and content that truly matter to them.

This approach could ease the burden of paying for channels that don't spark joy while still giving them access to their favorite shows and films.

We're also seeing the emergence of niche platforms that cater to specific audiences, creating a marketplace of options for those tired of the overwhelming but often disappointing cable model. While these platforms might be smaller, they offer unique programming that resonates deeply with particular groups, paving the way for a more engaging viewing experience. This evolving landscape hints at innovation and diversity, empowering viewers to shape their entertainment experiences in ways that truly reflect their interests.

As we navigate the changing world of television consumption, it's clear that the consumer choice dilemma is a mix of psychology, economics, and technology. The challenge lies not just in making choices but in making choices that feel right for each individual without causing overwhelm. Finding that sweet spot will be key in shaping the future of media, where the excitement of new possibilities matches the satisfaction of tailored experiences. What's on the horizon is an adventure filled with promise—one where viewers might discover that the secret to enjoying content isn't just the number of options available, but the quality and relevance of those options. The ability to curate a personal viewing experience is just the start of an exciting new chapter in the world of entertainment.

Media Consolidation

The media world has seen some dramatic changes in recent years, with waves of consolidation washing over the cable TV industry like a relentless tide. Mergers and acquisitions have reshaped who's who in the media scene, altering the game for viewers everywhere. To truly grasp what these consolidations mean, let's take a look at the timeline of major corporate moves and think about what they might mean for all of us.

The timeline reads like a gripping story filled with familiar names from the media landscape. One of the biggest mergers was AT&T's purchase of Time Warner in 2018 for an astonishing $85 billion. The goal? To combine content creation with distribution, hoping that working together would bring in new ways to make money. This strategy aimed to create a giant that could use its vast content library to boost AT&T's telecommunications business. The belief was that merging these two companies would set a new standard for delivering content in our increasingly digital world. But, as we've learned, it wasn't just about the cash; it was also about power and control in the market.

Then there's Disney's acquisition of 21st Century Fox, which wrapped up in 2019 for $71 billion. This deal didn't just give Disney access to a treasure trove of popular shows and movies—like "The Simpsons," "Avatar," and a host of

Marvel hits—but it also strengthened its position in the streaming world. By taking over a major competitor, Disney enhanced its offerings on Disney+ and became a stronger player against Netflix and Amazon Prime. For viewers, this has big implications: fewer companies are controlling a larger slice of content, which affects how varied and diverse our viewing options really are.

These mergers show a larger trend toward consolidation that has reshaped cable and media. Companies often pursue these moves to achieve economies of scale, gain more bargaining power with advertisers, and secure exclusive content that can't be found anywhere else. While this might seem like a smart business strategy, the reality for diversity and competition is much more concerning.

As a handful of companies gain control over most of the content produced and distributed, the range of available media has started to shrink. The rich variety that used to define cable television is giving way to a more uniform offering, where independent voices struggle to be heard amid the noise of corporate giants. Research indicates that consolidation leads to fewer distinct perspectives and ideas, which can limit creativity and innovation in content creation. When just a few companies dominate, the risk of producing cookie-cutter programming increases, as they tend to favor content that appeals to the broadest audience rather than taking risks on unique ideas.

The impact of this shift goes beyond just what's on our screens. Today, the television landscape is filled with franchises and sequels —just think of how many superhero movies or spin-off series we see! This corporate approach often prioritizes profits over artistic expression. Independent filmmakers and smaller studios are finding it harder to compete, making for a media environment that feels less diverse and lively. The rich variety of storytelling has, in some ways, been replaced by predictable formulas that favor financial success over originality.

On top of that, media consolidation has serious implications for cultural representation. When a small number of corporate leaders make decisions, the nuances and complexities of different cultures, communities, and narratives can easily be overlooked or ignored. This hinders the opportunity for a wide range of voices and stories to thrive, resulting in a media landscape that doesn't truly reflect the diverse experiences of its audience. If the content we watch doesn't connect with our realities, it creates a disconnect that can have wider societal effects.

As consolidation trends ramp up, there are growing concerns about the regulations surrounding these mergers. The Federal Communications Commission (FCC), the agency responsible for overseeing communications in the U.S., has faced a lot of scrutiny for its role in either supporting or limiting media consolidation. Over time, its policies have shifted—or, as some might argue, regressed—into a system that tends to favor larger corporations. The era of deregulation often operates under the belief that less oversight leads to more competition and innovation. However, many critics say it has allowed monopolistic practices to flourish without restraint.

Consider the relaxed ownership rules that let single companies control several media outlets in the same market. The thinking behind these changes is that a few larger companies can deliver content more effectively. But this raises serious questions about the availability of diverse viewpoints and local programming. When one company owns multiple news or entertainment channels in the same area, the risk of groupthink grows, which could lead to a homogenized flow of information that doesn't serve the public good.

In this tangled web of mergers and regulatory choices, the voice of the consumer often feels silenced. To better understand how these shifts impact viewers, qualitative research, including interviews, paints a complex picture. Many consumers express worries about the changing media landscape, especially regarding the diversity of content they can access. Some share their concerns about being funneled into a narrow set of options that cater to wide audiences, leaving out niche interests or culturally significant stories. There's also a noticeable shift in the perception of quality, with many viewers lamenting that their favorite shows are increasingly swapped out for formulaic reality series or overly commercialized programming that lacks the depth and complexity they crave.

Interestingly, some viewers are turning to streaming services and independent creators as alternatives to traditional cable. These platforms often focus on niche content that reflects specific communities and interests, encouraging creators to explore themes that might not fit into mainstream media. As audiences seek out these options, we must ask ourselves whether the traditional cable model can hold up in a time that increasingly values individuality and authenticity.

Looking ahead, the future of media consolidation brings both challenges and exciting possibilities. Will this trend continue to grow, or could we see a movement toward decentralization and independent content creation? We're starting to see signs of a counter-movement. With the rise of social media platforms, how content is shared is changing dramatically. Creators now have easier access to audiences without needing traditional gatekeepers, challenging the established norms in powerful ways. Platforms like YouTube and TikTok allow individuals to share their stories and perspectives, leading to a wide variety of content that reflects the many voices and experiences in our society.

The shift toward democratizing content creation and distribution opens up thrilling opportunities for the future of media. It could mark the beginning of a new era filled with diversity and creativity, giving audiences fresh viewpoints that the big media companies might overlook. The challenge will be making sure these independent voices can thrive in a landscape still largely dominated by large corporations. As we watch the ongoing tug-of-war between consolidation and independence, it remains to be seen whether we can move toward a more balanced media ecosystem—one that values both innovation and the richness of diverse storytelling.

The road ahead for media consolidation is full of questions. As consumers increasingly crave authenticity, representation, and variety, will the big companies listen to these needs, or will they cling to their tried-and-true formulas? The conversation about media consolidation and its impact on society will keep evolving, influencing not just what we watch, but also the very fabric of our cultural landscape. In this shifting environment, the fight for diverse voices and genuine narratives will be a key battleground, as audiences and creators navigate the complexities of an industry in transition.

CHAPTER 8: COMPETITION'S DOUBLE-EDGED SWORD

Gains from Initial Competition

Competition is a word that often sparks excitement and hope, conjuring images of lively markets filled with choices, all vying for the attention of eager customers. Picture yourself stepping into a bustling marketplace, where the air is rich with the aroma of fresh produce, artisanal goods, and cutting-edge products, each one trying to win you over. In the business world, this isn't just a dream; it's a reality, especially after waves of deregulation. When regulations are lifted, a flurry of changes can light up the competition in ways that feel both thrilling and transformative.

Let's take a closer look at the airline industry in the United States. This example shows just how energizing deregulation can be. Back in the late

1970s, the Airline Deregulation Act broke down the strict rules that had kept the industry in check. Before this groundbreaking law, air travel was a predictable but rather dull experience, with only a few airlines offering limited routes and steep prices. But after deregulation, the skies turned into a vibrant playground where innovation took flight alongside the airplanes. Routes expanded significantly; cities that were once overlooked suddenly found themselves connected to major hubs, making air travel possible for millions who had previously relied on road trips and train rides.

This surge in competition didn't just create more routes; it also led to a big drop in fares. Suddenly, flying was no longer just a luxury for the wealthy; it became an achievable dream for everyday Americans. Airlines, eager to attract passengers, rolled out enticing deals, loyalty programs, and a wider range of travel options. Consumers felt a new sense of power as they compared prices and services, prompting companies to keep innovating and improving.

The transformation in the airline industry exemplifies the many benefits that come when competition is allowed to thrive. Companies, hungry for their slice of the market, innovate continually—not just to grab attention, but to keep it. The spirit of entrepreneurship flourishes in such an environment. Small businesses are revitalized, ready to find their own unique spots in a world that rewards creativity and flexibility.

They seize the chance to offer distinctive services and products that set them apart from the bigger players.

Think about the tech sector, where startups often rise up to challenge established giants, driven by the thrilling idea of competition. The boom in software apps, mobile services, and online platforms has made technology accessible to everyone, allowing innovative entrepreneurs to shake up entire industries. Thanks to the digital age, small businesses can connect directly with customers like never before, utilizing social media and marketing strategies that were once only available to the well-funded.

This lively environment creates more than just choices; it encourages investment in technology and quality of service. Companies feel the need to spend on research and development, constantly pushing the boundaries of what's possible. This isn't just talk; research shows that industries with fierce competition invest more in innovative practices. Companies that rest on their past successes risk falling behind as their competitors seize the opportunity to lead.

Looking at the consumer experience during this exciting time is crucial. People enjoy an abundance of choices, often feeling a thrilling sense of freedom. They become active participants in a lively marketplace, not just passive recipients of goods and services. Their stories are filled with adventures—like spontaneous road trips made possible by a great airline fare. The joy of discovering new products that meet their needs is a direct result of the freedom that competition creates.

These changes in the marketplace also have personal stories behind them. Talking to everyday consumers reveals accounts of satisfaction and empowerment. One traveler remembers how a lower fare made it possible to visit family across the country more often, nurturing relationships that would have been too expensive before. Another person shares how the rise of budget airlines opened up travel options to places they once thought were out of reach, enriching their lives with unforgettable experiences.

For small businesses, the stories are equally inspiring. Entrepreneurs recount their journeys in a competitive landscape, driven by a passion to innovate and offer something unique. A local café owner describes how their vision of creating a community hub was inspired by the larger chains around them. The outcome? A vibrant local spot that not only thrives but also becomes a gathering place for people to connect.

Yet, with all the excitement that comes with competition, it's important to keep a clear view of its complexities. While the initial wave after deregulation typically leads to lower prices and improved services, it doesn't happen in isolation. The thrill of new competition can bring along unexpected outcomes as the landscape evolves over time.

In the rush of competition, some industries may experience what's known as "creative destruction." This is where new innovations replace outdated practices and products, leading to economic growth. But this can also reveal a more sobering truth: the vulnerability of new businesses facing off against bigger, established rivals. As companies race to innovate, the idea of "survival of the fittest" can take a harsh turn; not all will make it.

Additionally, while the benefits of competition are clear in the early days following deregulation, the path is rarely straightforward. The initial excitement can give way to hidden challenges. As firms compete for market share, they might resort to ruthless practices that, while good for consumers at first, can eventually lead to monopolistic behaviors. The landscape may shift from one filled with healthy competition to one dominated by just a few players, raising concerns about losing the very choices that once thrived.

Striking a balance between innovation and consolidation is vital. As we reflect on the gains that come from competition, it's essential to stay alert to the potential downsides of this double-edged sword. The joy of having more choices and the excitement of competition should not blind us to the risk that larger companies might swallow up the market, stifling the creativity that once flourished.

To truly understand this landscape, we need to listen to the stories of both consumers and businesses. Their experiences and insights provide a fuller view of the stakes involved in this competitive dance. It's this interplay between the thrill of choice and the risks of monopolistic practices that will ultimately shape the future of markets in a world where regulations are relaxed. The tale of competition is not just about winners and losers; it's about a rich and evolving narrative that encourages us to stay engaged, ask questions, and advocate for a marketplace that serves everyone.

As we think about the early gains from competition, we are reminded that this same competitive spirit can also lead to challenges that threaten the very energy it once brought. The ongoing relationship between deregulation and competition reminds us that every advantage gained comes with responsibilities and the potential for unexpected outcomes. This journey doesn't end with the initial excitement; it evolves into a more intricate story that deserves our attention.

Consolidation Trends

As the excitement of competition begins to fade, a more concerning trend emerges in the world of business: consolidation. The same energy that once invigorated markets and sparked entrepreneurship can gradually shift, favoring a select few while leaving many behind. The lively marketplaces that consumers once enjoyed may slowly turn into a barren landscape, dominated by a handful of powerful players. This trend is worth exploring because it reveals not only a change in the business environment but also the subtle decline of consumer choice.

Take a look at the telecommunications industry; it's a clear example of this worrying trend. Over the past few decades, we've seen a wave of mergers and acquisitions that have shrunk a once-thriving field of competitors into a tight-knit oligopoly. It's hard to believe there was a time when many providers vied for customers, each one trying to deliver better plans, innovative features, and excellent service. But as companies started to merge, everything changed. What was once a bustling marketplace filled with options and variety has been replaced by a situation where a few large corporations hold the reins, controlling the rules and the quality of service.

The numbers tell the story. Research from the Federal Communications Commission shows that the top four companies in the telecommunications market have seen their share soar from about 30% in the early 1990s to over 90% today. These staggering statistics point to a serious shift—not just in who's competing, but in how competition works. With fewer players in the game, innovation suffers and choices dwindle. Prices climb, service quality declines, and the sense of empowerment that consumers used to feel starts to disappear, leaving them feeling powerless against these corporate giants.

So, what drives this trend towards consolidation? One major reason is the regulatory environment that has shaped how companies operate over the years. Antitrust laws that once protected competition and discouraged monopolies have been gradually relaxed. Lawmakers, in their pursuit of economic efficiency and innovation, have loosened regulations that could have helped control this wave of consolidation. While the intention behind deregulation was to encourage competition and lower prices, the result has often been the opposite —a concentration of market power that harms consumers.

A clear example of this is the merger between Sprint and T-Mobile. At first, this merger was seen as a way to create a stronger competitor against the market leaders, AT&T and Verizon. However, as many analysts warned, the outcome was a rapid decline in competition. Consumers soon found their options narrowing, and it wasn't just about losing a brand name; it meant losing competitive pricing and diverse choices. The promise of improved service or lower rates tends to vanish after these mergers, leaving consumers facing a harsh reality with fewer choices.

This trend toward consolidation isn't limited to telecommunications. The financial services industry has undergone a similar transformation. Once filled with regional banks and institutions that served local needs, it has shifted to a landscape dominated by a few large players, each offering very similar products. In this scenario, competition dwindles, and consumers find themselves with limited options for banking services. The days of walking into a local bank and receiving personalized service tailored to individual needs are long gone. Instead, consumers are met with generic solutions that prioritize corporate profit over personal attention.

The consequences of consolidation go beyond what consumers experience; they also extend to the job market. As companies merge and grow larger, they often look to cut costs to boost profits, leading to job losses and weaker bargaining power for workers. The logic behind this is simple: with fewer firms in the market, workers have fewer job options. This shift in power tilts toward employers, resulting in stagnant wages and declining benefits. This creates a cycle where the few big companies can set terms that were once negotiated in a more balanced environment.

Psychological factors play a part in this trend as well. Economies of scale become important here. Bigger companies can often produce goods and services at lower costs than their smaller competitors, giving them a significant advantage. As these larger companies gain more power, their size can become appealing to consumers. After all, who wouldn't want the convenience and reliability that comes with dealing with a big name? This is especially true in industries where network effects are strong, like technology platforms. The more people use a particular service, the more valuable it becomes, creating a cycle that attracts consumers while pushing smaller competitors aside.

While consolidation may appear to be a neat solution to the challenges of competition, its effects can be severe. The excitement of consumer choice and innovation, once hallmarks of healthy markets, can quickly fade under the weight of monopolistic practices. The empowerment that customers felt while navigating a diverse marketplace gives way to frustration and a sense of helplessness. As a few select companies dominate the market, the lively competition turns into a discouraging standoff where quality and choice plummet.

To truly grasp this issue, we need to dig deeper. We must explore the complex relationships between different market players and how these dynamics change as consolidation occurs. Understanding these interactions reminds us that markets are not just mechanical systems; they are living ecosystems shaped by people, regulations, and economic realities. Finding the right balance between competition and consolidation is a complicated challenge that requires thoughtful engagement from everyone involved.

The experiences of consumers, small businesses, and employees are vital to this broader conversation. As we try to understand the effects of consolidation, listening to their stories becomes crucial. Consumers can share their firsthand experiences of navigating a world with fewer choices, while businesses can shed light on the difficulties they face in an environment increasingly dominated by a few giants. Similarly, workers can discuss how consolidation impacts their jobs and security. Their collective voices highlight the importance of staying aware as we navigate our ever-changing economic landscape.

Ultimately, understanding consolidation trends is more than just an academic exercise; it's a key part of addressing the future of our markets. The delicate balance between competition and consolidation needs careful attention. As we witness these trends unfold, we should remain active participants, questioning the decisions made by those in power and advocating for a fairer approach that protects consumer choice and preserves the marketplace's integrity. The story of competition, with its ups and downs, serves as a reminder that we must stay vigilant to ensure our economic systems serve everyone, not just a select few.

Impacts on Innovation

As the business world evolves, understanding the shifts in competition and consolidation becomes vital, especially regarding innovation. In this intricate landscape, the link between market structure and innovation is crucial. It helps us see the different results that can emerge from competitive practices. At first, competition serves as a key driver for innovation, motivating companies to push boundaries and create new products and services. But as the competitive scene shifts towards consolidation, a more concerning story often unfolds—one where the spark of innovation hangs in the balance and may even slide toward stagnation.

To illustrate this, let's look closely at the pharmaceutical industry, a field that perfectly showcases the mixed effects of competition and consolidation. In the early stages of drug development, the industry thrives on competition. Companies are pushed to innovate, striving to create groundbreaking drugs and treatments to gain an edge in the market. However, as smaller firms emerge, a pattern of consolidation can take hold, often resulting in larger companies acquiring their promising competitors. The logic is straightforward: why take a chance on a potentially risky innovation when you can simply purchase it? This not only narrows the pathways for innovation but also creates an atmosphere where major players can suppress competition through aggressive patenting strategies and market dominance.

One of the most concerning effects of this consolidation is the chilling impact it can have on smaller innovators. When a big company with deep pockets and a vast patent portfolio buys a smaller competitor, the very innovation that could have led to a groundbreaking treatment might be buried, perhaps never to see the light of day. The patenting strategies used can build significant barriers for emerging companies, making it harder for them to navigate the complex legal landscape surrounding these innovations. It's a tough situation—where the fierce competition that once drove creativity is gradually replaced by a monopolistic culture that favors existing profits over fresh ideas.

The famous economist Joseph Schumpeter introduced the term "creative destruction" to explain this cycle of innovation and renewal. This idea highlights that competition can push companies to innovate energetically, often at the expense of less efficient rivals, which eventually leads to new products and services that disrupt the market. It's this lively competition that can ignite a surge of new ideas and inventions. However, in the aftermath of consolidation, this cycle can break down. When fewer firms control the market, the drive to innovate can fade. After all, why spend heavily on uncertain innovations when a company can continue to profit from well-established products?

Investment in research and development is another area where the impact of consolidation shows up clearly. Studies indicate that larger firms, once they reach a certain size, may lean towards the safety of existing revenue streams rather than venture into the unpredictable world of new ideas. This cautious mindset stifles the very innovation that competition is supposed to encourage. The alarming truth is that as consolidated firms focus on maximizing profits from what they already offer, the larger landscape suffers. New advancements that could change lives or transform industries might linger in obscurity, victims of an environment where risk-taking is overshadowed by the lure of immediate financial rewards.

Even the tech sector, often seen as the poster child for innovation, is not safe from the downsides of consolidation. Initially, the tech world buzzed with creativity, with numerous startups eager to make their mark. Entrepreneurs flourished, launching apps and platforms that changed how we communicate, work, and live. Yet, in recent years, this spirit of innovation faces serious challenges. Major players, boosted by their size and influence, frequently choose to acquire budding companies rather than allow them to grow independently. While these acquisitions can sometimes lead to beneficial collaborations, they also risk extinguishing the independent innovation that helped these companies shine in the first place.

Take social media platforms as an example. The field has become increasingly concentrated, with a handful of companies dominating vast user bases. When a startup captures the public's attention, it's often more likely to be acquired by a larger competitor rather than competing on its merits. In such cases, the innovative spark that fueled the startup's success can be dulled by the corporate bureaucracy that comes with being absorbed into a larger entity. This raises pressing questions about the future of innovation in an arena that has become less competitive and more consolidated.

Government policy also plays a crucial role in either encouraging or hindering innovation in consolidated markets. Regulations can either stifle competition or create a fertile ground for creativity. A prime example can be found in the contrasting environments of innovation hubs like Silicon Valley compared to sectors marked by heavy consolidation. In Silicon Valley, a culture that encourages competition, risk-taking, and collaboration has created an ecosystem perfect for innovation. Startups thrive on venture capital support, allowing them to explore groundbreaking ideas, and even if they fail, the lessons learned often lead to future successes.

On the flip side, consider the healthcare sector. While it's crucial for advancements to occur, it's also one of the most regulated and consolidated areas of the economy. The regulatory hurdles and the tendency for large corporations to dominate this space can stifle smaller innovators who lack the resources or connections to navigate its complexities. The outcome? A slower pace of innovation, fewer breakthroughs, and less competition, ultimately affecting the quality and accessibility of healthcare for consumers.

This contrast between different industries serves as a reminder that innovation isn't just about having smart people involved; it needs the right environment to grow and develop. When companies feel secure in their market position, the push to innovate can lessen. Keeping competition alive is vital for keeping the creative wheels turning. It's crucial to understand how failing to maintain competition can leave lasting impacts on an industry and society at large.

To illustrate these concepts more clearly, let's examine examples of successful innovation hubs alongside those affected by consolidation. Silicon Valley, as mentioned, has become a symbol of tech innovation. Here, the atmosphere thrives on collaboration, competition, and a free exchange of ideas. Startups often work side by side, sparking inspiration and a sense of camaraderie. This dynamic environment remains a hotbed for new ideas, with far-reaching implications beyond the local area.

In contrast, think about the traditional media industry. The consolidation of major news outlets has led to a concentration of power and a sameness in news coverage. The lively debates that once flourished, fueled by a multitude of independent voices, have increasingly been muted by a few dominant players. As innovation stalls, so does the public's access to diverse viewpoints, creating an echo chamber that can undermine the very foundations of democracy. The drop in competition leads not only to fewer options for consumers but also to a reduced capacity for critical discourse, which ultimately stifles innovation.

By comparing these case studies, we can gain valuable insights into the important relationship between market structure and innovation. We learn that a lively competitive environment isn't just a backdrop; it's a driving force that fuels creativity and inspires the kinds of innovations that can transform entire industries. When consolidation happens, the motivations shift, and the essential cycle of innovation begins to stumble.

As we take a step back to look at these dynamics, it becomes clear that the challenge lies in creating a balanced approach that encourages innovation while keeping harmful consolidation in check. Policymakers must thoughtfully weigh the effects of mergers and acquisitions, considering the potential advantages against the threats to competition and innovation. The right regulatory framework can be vital in protecting an ecosystem where new ideas can flourish alongside established players.

In our constantly changing economic

landscape, grasping the intricacies of competition, consolidation, and innovation is key. As we explore these connections, we need to stay alert in advocating for a marketplace that benefits not just a select few but the wider population. Supporting competition, nurturing emerging innovators, and creating a dynamic environment will lead to an economy that is resilient, adaptable, and genuinely innovative.

With this understanding, we're ready to face the future of innovation with a critical eye, knowing that the choices we make today will echo in the halls of commerce for years to come. By keeping the conversation going and acknowledging the importance of competition in driving innovation, we can navigate toward a more fair and innovative economic landscape. As the story unfolds, it's evident that the twin forces of competition and consolidation will continue to shape our markets, reminding us of the delicate balance we must strive to maintain for the good of everyone.

CHAPTER 9: UNINTENDED OUTCOMES

Economic Volatility

Economic history is full of significant moments—events that signal a shift, marking the move from one set of rules to another. In this context, deregulation emerges as a hot topic, sparking lively discussions and differing opinions. The idea of free markets and unrestricted competition sounds appealing, but the reality often tells a different story. It can lead to surprising outcomes that even experienced economists might not foresee. This brings us to a crucial point: when oversight disappears, economic volatility can take hold, as shown by historical examples that resonate with us today.

The 2008 financial crisis is a vivid example that remains etched in our minds, a clear reminder of what can happen when regulations are loosened in favor of hands-off policies. It's important to explore the details of this crisis—how it unfolded and what factors made it so severe. One major issue was the repeal of the Glass-Steagall Act in 1999, a law created during the Great Depression to limit the dangers of blending commercial and investment banking. With this repeal, financial institutions were free to dive into a range of activities without the oversight that once kept them accountable.

Looking back at the lead-up to the crisis, we can see that many factors created the perfect storm for disaster. As commercial banks stepped into investment banking territory, they took on risks that had previously been kept in check. Fueled by the lure of quick profits, these institutions began crafting complicated financial products, like mortgage-backed securities and derivatives, which were hard to grasp for both investors and regulators. The outcome was a dangerous mix of excessive risk-taking and a lack of transparency, eventually leading to a financial meltdown.

The housing market, a key part of the American economy, was at the center of this chaos. Banks relaxed their lending standards in their chase for profit, giving loans to borrowers who had questionable credit histories—people who, under stricter regulations, would have been seen as too risky. This situation sparked the subprime mortgage crisis, which set off a wave of defaults that spread through the financial system. The fallout was devastating: banks and financial institutions crumbled, credit markets seized up, and millions of Americans lost their homes. The painful truth was that easing regulations had allowed the very practices that caused this systemic failure to flourish.

But the financial sector isn't the only area that faced turmoil when regulations faded away. If we look at the airline industry, we find a similar story where short-term gains were overshadowed by long-term instability. The Airline Deregulation Act of 1978 was praised as a groundbreaking policy meant to boost competition, lower fares, and improve services for travelers. At first glance, things seemed to go well: ticket prices dropped, new routes appeared, and many new airlines sprang up to meet the growing demand.

However, beneath this shiny surface, economic volatility was brewing. With the removal of restrictions on routes and pricing, airlines began competing fiercely with each other, sparking a downward spiral on ticket prices. While passengers enjoyed lower fares, the airlines themselves struggled to maintain sustainable financial models. The rising costs of operating flights, combined with fluctuating fuel prices, created financial challenges that many airlines couldn't handle. The inevitable consequences became clear as several major carriers went bankrupt in the years that followed, including some iconic names in aviation.

The effects of the Airline Deregulation Act

extended beyond just the financial troubles of the airlines. The sweeping changes led to job losses throughout the sector, as airlines cut costs by streamlining operations and laying off staff. Airports in smaller markets, which had once been busy hubs, found themselves without service as airlines shifted their focus to more profitable routes, leaving entire regions underserved. What began as a promise of competition turned into a tough reality: while some airlines thrived, many others struggled, leading to fewer choices for consumers and a decline in overall service quality.

These two examples—the financial crisis and the airline industry—illustrate a clear pattern: deregulation, though often hailed for its potential to unleash market forces and lower costs, can also create economic volatility that undermines the goals it aimed to achieve. Quick wins can transform into long-term challenges as industries wrestle with the fallout from reduced oversight and an unyielding focus on profit. The effects of these choices ripple out, influencing not just businesses but also employees, consumers, and entire communities.

As we reflect on these events, the insights we gain are crucial for future policymakers. Finding the right balance between encouraging competition and maintaining stability is a tricky dance that requires careful attention and foresight. While the lure of deregulation may promise efficiency and innovation, the consequences of allowing market forces to run wild remind us of the delicate relationship between regulation and economic health. The path ahead calls for thoughtful consideration of the impact of removing regulatory protections, as industries continue to find their way between risk and reward.

With these lessons in mind, we face a key question: how can society find a way to encourage innovation and competition while still protecting the public good? Moving forward, it's vital to create regulatory frameworks that can adapt to the changing landscape of industries. Striking this balance will be crucial to avoid repeating the mistakes of the past and to ensure that the lessons learned from these case studies lead us toward a more stable economic future for everyone.

Ethical Oversights

The relationship between regulation and industry can often play out in unsettling ways. While easing regulations might spark innovation and competition, it can also compromise ethical standards. When profit becomes the main goal, the critical duty that companies have toward public safety and the environment can be pushed aside. This reality was tragically highlighted by the Deepwater Horizon oil spill, a disaster that exposed the severe risks of cutting back on regulations.

The Deepwater Horizon incident, which happened on April 20, 2010, stands as a vivid example of what can occur when oversight is neglected. The explosion of the offshore drilling rig not only led to the heartbreaking loss of 11 crew members but also released millions of barrels of crude oil into the Gulf of Mexico. This event became one of the worst environmental disasters in U.S. history. The effects of the spill were not just confined to the area around the accident; they rippled throughout the Gulf Coast, impacting marine life, local economies, and public health for years.

To fully appreciate the implications of this disaster, it's important to consider the regulatory backdrop that existed before it. In the years leading up to the spill, the oil and gas industry enjoyed a significant relaxation of safety oversight. During the Bush administration, policies were put in place that favored deregulation and promoted domestic energy production over stringent safety protocols. This shift fostered a culture within companies like BP, where the focus shifted from safety measures to financial gains and efficiency. This created an atmosphere where businesses felt they could operate without strict regulations.

The moments before the explosion now serve as a painful reminder of industrial negligence. Many safety checks were ignored, and crucial information about the well's integrity was either overlooked or misrepresented. It's clear now that the reckless decisions made leading up to the disaster prioritized profit over safety. BP and its partners, including Transocean and Halliburton, chose to skimp on vital safety protocols, putting cost-cutting ahead of what was needed to protect the environment and human lives. This behavior reflects a troubling trend in the industry, where the drive for profit overtook the moral responsibility to safeguard the public and the planet.

While this story is sobering, it also echoes in other areas, like the food industry. In recent years, we've seen alarming foodborne illness outbreaks tied to relaxed inspection standards. The relationship between deregulation and food safety shows just how complicated the consequences can be when oversight is lessened.

Take, for example, the heartbreaking events of the 2006 E. coli outbreak linked to fresh spinach, which resulted in hundreds of illnesses and several deaths. Investigations revealed that the spinach became contaminated due to weak inspection practices and insufficient oversight of farming methods. In their rush to increase profits, growers may have ignored crucial safety protocols, allowing tainted products to reach consumers. This incident, much like the Deepwater Horizon spill, highlighted the tragic consequences of placing profit above safety and raises difficult questions about producers' ethical duties to ensure the safety of their goods.

As we keep following the story of foodborne

illnesses, it becomes evident that the blame doesn't solely lie with the growers. We also need to look at the role of regulatory agencies, like the Food and Drug Administration (FDA) and the United States Department of Agriculture (USDA). Their ability to enforce safety standards has been weakened over the years due to budget cuts and political pressure to reduce government involvement. This situation has created an environment where companies can operate with less accountability, resulting in disastrous effects for consumers.

The ethical oversights that come with deregulation bring up vital questions about the responsibilities of corporations and the regulatory bodies that supervise them. It's important to examine these challenges through the lens of ethics, as the balance between profit and public safety can be difficult to strike. Business ethics often highlights the significance of stakeholder theory, which suggests that companies should consider the interests of all parties involved —including consumers, employees, and the community—rather than simply focusing on maximizing shareholder profits.

Talking to industry experts and ethical thinkers sheds light on the complicated moral issues that arise when regulations are loosened. As the drive for profit and efficiency takes center stage, ethical considerations are often pushed to the side. The tragedies of the Deepwater Horizon spill and food safety outbreaks reveal a troubling truth: when profit is prioritized without oversight, it can lead to catastrophic results.

Experts stress the need for a strong ethical framework within businesses, one that goes beyond just following legal rules. This framework should prioritize the health of consumers and the environment, recognizing that ethical oversight isn't just a formality but a key part of a healthy society. The pressing question becomes: how can we align corporate ethics with public well-being?

Ethics forms the foundation of a fair and just society. As we look at the complicated landscape of deregulation and its effects, it's clear we can't overlook the ethical responsibilities of businesses. The role of regulatory bodies is equally vital; they must not only enforce existing laws but also adapt proactively to the evolving landscape of industries, ensuring that ethical considerations stay at the forefront of decision-making.

These examples make the ethical challenges of deregulation painfully clear. The price of prioritizing profit over safety can lead to disastrous consequences for individuals, communities, and the environment. The stories of the Deepwater Horizon spill and foodborne illness outbreaks are strong reminders of the need to recommit to ethical oversight.

Ultimately, seeking profit shouldn't mean sacrificing public safety. The lessons learned from these disasters should inspire action from both corporations and regulators. The business landscape is always changing, and as we continue to see the unintended effects of deregulation, we must reaffirm the importance of ethical oversight. Striking a balance between economic goals and ethical responsibilities isn't just a nice idea; it's something we must work toward in our efforts for progress.

As we reflect on the past and the lessons it offers, we remember that the stakes are high, and the duty to protect public welfare falls on all of us. By nurturing a culture that prioritizes ethics and accountability, we can create a space where innovation and public safety can thrive together, ultimately benefiting society as a whole. The pursuit of profit doesn't have to come with a price; instead, it can align with the principles of responsibility and care that define a truly flourishing community.

Regulatory Voids

In a world full of constant change and new ideas, the lack of strong rules and regulations has become a major concern. The technology industry, known for its ability to shake up traditional markets, shows how these regulatory gaps can lead to unfair practices and inequalities that affect everyone. While companies like Uber and Airbnb have transformed how we think about getting around and finding places to stay, they've also exposed serious flaws in how we protect workers and consumers. This gap between rapid innovation and necessary regulations creates openings for risks that people often don't realize until it's too late.

Consider Uber as an example. What started as a groundbreaking way to get a ride quickly has turned into a complex situation. The convenience of hailing a car with a few taps on your smartphone hides a reality where drivers, often treated as independent contractors, miss out on the benefits and protections that regular employees receive. In the rush to embrace this new way of working, regulatory agencies have struggled to keep up, leaving drivers without important safety nets. Many have shared stories of long hours, low pay, and no health benefits, all while being treated more like tools than human beings. In this environment, the gig economy flourishes in a space where the focus is on flexibility instead of stability.

Airbnb tells a similar story. This platform has changed the hospitality scene by allowing people to rent out their homes to travelers. While this innovation has opened up new ways for many to earn extra income, it has also caused serious issues for local housing markets. In some cities, the rise of short-term rentals has pushed up housing prices and made it harder for residents to find affordable homes, as properties meant for long-term living are transformed into profitable vacation spots. The lack of clear regulations to manage these changes has put communities at risk, raising important questions about the rights of homeowners compared to the needs of local residents. The effects are significant, as neighborhoods once known for their unique character risk becoming uniform tourist traps, losing the culture and community spirit that makes them special.

The unregulated nature of the gig economy and the rise of short-term rentals highlights a growing need for rules that can keep up with the fast pace of technology. Without proactive steps, the advantages of innovation can easily turn into exploitation, where profit becomes more important than people. This calls for a rethinking of what regulation should look like in a world where technology is changing so quickly. Instead of just aiming to limit innovation, the goal should be to create a space where it can flourish in a responsible way.

To grasp the importance of effective regulations, it's crucial to recognize that technology doesn't operate in isolation; it exists within a complex mix of societal values, economic pressures, and ethical issues. As industries change, the policies that guide them must evolve as well. This means that regulatory bodies should take a forward-looking approach, one that anticipates the potential harms that come with new technologies rather than just responding to them after problems arise. It's not just about creating rules; it involves working with everyone affected—

from consumers to workers to business leaders—to understand the different viewpoints that shape our landscape.

Failing to take a proactive approach to regulation can lead to serious problems. For instance, when Uber drivers don't have access to basic labor rights, it opens the door to unfair practices that can leave people struggling financially. Similarly, when Airbnb rentals grow without limits, it can disrupt local communities and push up housing costs, making it harder for residents to find affordable living spaces. These challenges reveal not just the shortcomings of individual companies, but also systemic weaknesses in the regulatory frameworks that shape our economy and society.

Moreover, the increasing use of data-driven technologies adds another layer of difficulty to the discussion about regulatory gaps. The rise of big data and artificial intelligence offers great opportunities but also raises significant concerns about privacy and surveillance. As companies collect more personal data than ever, the chances of misuse rise, leaving consumers to navigate a digital world with few safeguards. The lack of strong data privacy regulations has created a situation where individuals often have little say in how their information is collected, used, or shared. This not only puts their personal data at risk but also erodes trust in the technologies that are meant to enhance their lives.

The challenges stemming from these regulatory voids underscore the urgent need for a shift in how we approach regulation. Rather than seeing it as an obstacle to progress, we should view it as a vital tool to ensure that innovation benefits everyone. This means prioritizing public welfare, worker rights, and consumer protection as key aspects of regulatory design. By engaging with the realities of technological growth, we can establish frameworks that not only allow innovation to thrive but also protect against its potential downsides.

Regulatory bodies should do more than enforce rules; they must also cultivate an environment where ethical considerations are front and center. This requires teamwork among lawmakers, industry leaders, and community members to create policies that meet the diverse needs and concerns of all stakeholders. As industries continue to change, our approach to regulation must adapt, ensuring that it remains effective in addressing the challenges posed by rapid innovation.

At the end of the day, the gaps in regulation reflect wider societal values and priorities. If we let innovation happen without adequate oversight, we risk creating a future where profits come before people and communities. The demand for comprehensive and forward-thinking regulations has never been clearer, as the costs of inaction can be significant and long-lasting. The future of work, housing, and privacy shouldn't be dictated by regulatory gaps but by a commitment to fostering environments where innovation can grow responsibly.

As we navigate this intricate landscape, it's crucial to remember that regulation isn't just a bureaucratic hurdle; it's a way to build a fair and just society. By supporting strong regulatory frameworks, we can ensure that the advantages of technological progress are shared by all, rather than concentrated in the hands of a few. The challenge is not to stifle innovation but to direct it toward the common good, paving the way for a future where everyone has the chance to succeed. In this context, the conversation about regulatory voids isn't just about rules; it's about the core principles that shape our economic and social systems. Now is the time to rethink the role of regulation, recognizing its importance in creating a future that balances progress with responsibility.

CHAPTER 10: THE FUTURE OF BALANCE

Policy Proposals for a Balanced Approach

In the world of economics, where competition and regulation often move in a complex dance, it's important to create a system that works for everyone involved. Striving for balance—finding that tricky middle ground between market freedom and the oversight we need—is central to making effective policies. Right now, as we navigate through rapid technological changes and complicated economic conditions, it's more important than ever to consider how we can build frameworks that encourage this balance. This isn't just a theoretical exercise; it's a pressing need in our fast-evolving society.

At the heart of any meaningful reform in regulation lies the need to identify guiding principles for policymakers. These key ideas—transparency, accountability, and responsiveness—aren't just fancy terms thrown around in meetings; they form the foundation of solid regulations. Transparency helps everyone make informed choices in the marketplace, while accountability ensures that those in power are answerable for their actions. Additionally, being responsive to changes in the market acknowledges how industries evolve and highlights the necessity for regulations to adapt to new realities.

Let's take a look at the telecommunications sector to see these principles in action. Over the past few decades, this industry has changed dramatically due to deregulation. The introduction of competition has resulted in more choices for consumers and sparked technological advances. However, without a regulatory framework to ensure accountability and transparency, this shift could have led to monopolies that hinder competition. Policymakers understood the need to maintain oversight while embracing deregulation, resulting in systems that promote competition and protect consumers from unfair practices.

If we broaden our view beyond telecommunications, we can find many examples that showcase successful regulatory frameworks in different sectors. The financial industry, particularly in the wake of the 2008 financial crisis, tells a powerful story of how regulations can be adjusted for better balance. After the crisis, laws like the Dodd-Frank Act were introduced to protect consumers while ensuring economic stability. By imposing stricter requirements on financial institutions and ensuring clearer information in financial transactions, the law aimed to fill the accountability gap that contributed to the crisis.

These examples highlight a common theme: effective regulatory frameworks can blend the benefits of deregulation with the need for oversight. They demonstrate that when competition is managed well, it can drive innovation and satisfy consumers without compromising the greater good. As we look closely at these frameworks, we see that the insights gained can guide the development of policies in other industries facing rapid change, such as healthcare, transportation, and energy.

One of the most exciting trends in regulatory practices is the emergence of innovative models, like regulatory sandboxes. Imagine a safe space where startups and innovators can test out new ideas and technologies without the fear of harsh penalties from regulators. This concept, which started in the fintech sector, is now being applied across various fields to encourage innovation while still ensuring accountability.

By allowing businesses to operate within a controlled environment, regulators can observe how these new ideas affect consumers and the market in real-time. This approach not only provides valuable insights for regulatory bodies but also gives businesses the flexibility to adapt their offerings to better meet consumer needs. The success of these models relies heavily on the collaboration between regulators and innovators, highlighting the significance of including different voices in the regulatory process.

Involving a wide range of stakeholders —businesses, consumers, advocacy groups, and policymakers—is crucial for building a balanced regulatory landscape. By creating an atmosphere of collaboration, regulatory bodies can tap into the shared knowledge and experiences of everyone involved, ensuring that regulations are relevant and serve the public interest.

Some effective strategies for engaging stakeholders include holding public consultations, organizing workshops, and facilitating joint problem-solving sessions. By fostering open dialogue, regulators can gain a deeper understanding of the challenges and opportunities faced by different groups. This collaborative mindset can lead to co-created policy solutions that are not only effective but also widely accepted, making it easier for everyone to follow the rules.

The journey to find a balanced regulatory strategy isn't straightforward; it's a dynamic mix of principles, real-world examples, innovative methods, and collaboration among stakeholders. As we think about the future, it's clear that to harness the potential of deregulation while protecting the public good, we must craft policies that reflect the complexities of today's economy.

In this light, we might ask ourselves: how can we ensure that our regulatory frameworks keep up with the rapid pace of innovation? This question prompts us to consider the need for continuous evaluation and adaptation in regulatory practices. It encourages us to imagine a future where regulations are flexible and able to respond to the constantly changing landscape of industries and technologies.

The path to achieving a balanced regulatory approach is ongoing. By learning from our past and embracing new models, we must stay committed to principles that prioritize transparency, accountability, and responsiveness. This commitment will help us create an environment where innovation can thrive, competition can grow, and public welfare is safeguarded. The future holds great promise for a regulatory landscape that not only supports progress but also protects the rights and interests of everyone involved.

As we look ahead, we are guided by the lessons of history, the achievements of current frameworks, and the daring innovations on the horizon. Balancing the complexities of regulation and deregulation will require us to remain agile, informed, and open to collaboration. While the challenges are significant, the potential benefits —an economy that fosters creativity, innovation, and fairness—are even greater.

Historical Lessons: What the Past Teaches Us

The story of regulation is packed with both warnings and enlightening examples that give us important lessons about how to govern. This exploration isn't just a trip down memory lane; it's a chance to learn from the successes and failures of past regulations. As we face a world that changes quickly and is full of new technology, the insights we draw from historical events can help today's policymakers navigate the challenges of our evolving economy.

One standout example in the history of regulation is the deregulation of the airline industry in the late 1970s. The Airline Deregulation Act of 1978 brought about a major change in how air travel was managed in the United States. Before this law, the airline industry was heavily regulated, with strict controls over fares and routes. The idea behind this oversight was to provide stability and protect consumers from the potential dangers of monopolies.

However, as time went on, it became clear that this system had its flaws. High prices, limited choices, and poor customer service left many travelers feeling frustrated and looking for better options. Supporters of deregulation argued that allowing more competition would shake things up, resulting in lower fares and better service. Their hopes were realized when the government removed restrictions on routes and prices, paving the way for new airlines to enter the market.

The results were remarkable. Airlines, once constrained by strict regulations, began to thrive in a competitive environment. This shift encouraged innovation and efficiency, ultimately benefiting consumers. Fares dropped significantly, leading to a surge in air travel that positively impacted the economy. New airlines emerged, each trying to capture market share by offering unique services, discounts, and fresh ways to engage with customers. The changes in the airline industry showed us that smart deregulation can lead to great outcomes.

But this historical moment also comes with important warnings. While competition increased, the new market conditions brought about challenges that needed attention. Many of the new airlines operated on very thin profit margins, causing some to cut corners on safety and reliability. Furthermore, as major carriers merged in the following years, questions arose about the long-term effects of deregulation. The rise of large airlines, while initially praised for creating stronger companies, ended up reducing competition on certain routes and, in some cases, leading to higher fares.

Another significant moment to consider is the financial sector leading up to the 2008 financial crisis. The late 1990s and early 2000s saw major financial deregulation, such as the repeal of the Glass-Steagall Act, which had kept commercial banking separate from investment banking. Supporters believed that tearing down these walls would lead to more efficiency and growth in financial services.

What happened instead was a series of devastating failures that exposed the dangers of unchecked market forces. The rise of complicated financial products, like mortgage-backed securities, combined with a lack of oversight, created a perfect storm of risk that spiraled out of control. When the housing bubble burst, it caused widespread foreclosures and the collapse of major banks. The impact was severe, affecting not only the banking industry but also countless everyday people whose lives were forever changed.

In the aftermath of this crisis, the lessons were painfully clear: deregulation without proper safeguards can lead to market chaos and public harm. The response to the crisis sparked a shift in how we think about regulation. The Dodd-Frank Wall Street Reform and Consumer Protection Act, passed in 2010, aimed to create a new regulatory framework designed to reduce systemic risks, enhance protections for consumers, and hold financial institutions accountable.

As we look back at these historical moments, a clear pattern starts to emerge. Effective regulatory systems find a balance—one that encourages competition while ensuring protections are in place for the public. The airline industry's changes highlight the benefits of deregulation but also remind us of the need for careful oversight. Similarly, the financial crisis illustrates the dire consequences that can result when regulators fail to protect economic stability.

Recognizing these patterns provides valuable insights for today's policymakers. It's important to adopt a mindset that values flexibility and foresight as market conditions change. History shows us that regulatory systems shouldn't be set in stone; they need to be regularly reviewed and updated to tackle new challenges and seize opportunities. This means working together with a variety of stakeholders —business leaders, consumer advocates, and regulatory agencies—to create an environment that encourages innovation while protecting the public.

As we deal with the complexities of our digital age, which is shaped by rapid technological growth and shifts in consumer habits, the need for a flexible regulatory framework becomes even more pressing. The growth of the gig economy, the rise of financial technology, and the introduction of artificial intelligence all present new challenges and opportunities that require a thoughtful understanding of regulation. Policymakers must learn from past experiences to create systems that are not only responsive but also strong enough to handle unexpected disruptions.

One important takeaway from history is that regulation doesn't have to hinder innovation; instead, it can help drive progress. For example, regulatory sandboxes have emerged as a new way to encourage experimentation in safe settings. These spaces allow startups and innovators to test new ideas with real customers while giving regulators insights into market behaviors. The collaborative nature of these initiatives shows how regulations can be designed to promote growth while keeping accountability in mind.

History is filled with stories of regulatory successes and failures that remind us of the importance of learning from the past. Each case, from the success of airline deregulation to the cautionary tale of the financial crisis, serves as a reminder that careful oversight is vital for fostering a thriving market. The lessons of history urge us to reflect on our current regulatory strategies and to stay alert as things change.

To translate these historical lessons into effective policies, it's crucial to build a culture of ongoing evaluation and reform. Policymakers should set up systems for regularly reviewing existing regulations and be open to making changes based on new economic conditions and technological advancements. This iterative approach creates a lively regulatory environment that meets the needs of both consumers and businesses.

In addition, including a wide range of

voices in the regulatory process is key to creating effective policies. By listening to input from different sectors, regulators can better understand the challenges and opportunities within the market. This collaborative approach ensures that regulations are informed by data and also reflect the realities of those they affect.

The lessons of history aren't just theoretical; they have real implications for our future. As we find ourselves at the intersection of innovation and regulation, we have a chance to shape a system that balances the benefits of deregulation with the necessary elements of oversight. The journey ahead may be filled with obstacles, but by taking the lessons of the past to heart, we can carve out a path that welcomes progress while protecting the public good.

In our pursuit of a balanced regulatory framework, we should embrace the idea that regulation isn't an obstacle to growth, but a supporter of a healthy economy. The historical lessons we've explored serve as a vital reminder to remain watchful in our commitment to oversight while also celebrating the positive effects of thoughtful deregulation. The relationship between regulation and innovation is a delicate balance that requires careful attention to ensure that both can thrive.

As we look ahead, let's be guided by the principles of adaptability, foresight, and collaboration that arise from our historical insights. By embracing these values, we can create a regulatory framework that not only supports innovation but also protects us from the risks of an unregulated market. The lessons from history are clear: when we learn from our past, we equip ourselves with the tools needed to build a more stable and prosperous future for everyone.

Evolving Regulations: Innovation Meets Protection

The rapid growth of technology is changing the way we live, work, and interact at an incredible speed. In this whirlwind of change, the role of regulation becomes crucial—not just as a set of rules to follow, but as a partner that helps guide innovation. The relationship between new technologies—like artificial intelligence, blockchain, and biotechnology—and the laws that govern them is complex and requires both flexibility and a willingness to adapt. We're beginning to see that regulations can't just stay the same; they need to evolve, adjusting to the fast-paced market while also protecting the public's interests.

Technology isn't just transforming existing fields; it's also creating entire industries that didn't exist before. Take artificial intelligence, for example. In just a few years, AI has shifted from a specialized area of study to a major force influencing everything from healthcare and finance to manufacturing and education. This quick change calls for a new way of thinking about traditional regulatory systems, which were designed for a different time—one that didn't have the same complexities brought on by AI. The real challenge is to find a way to encourage innovation while also making sure that ethical standards, data privacy, and security are upheld.

Now let's look at the blockchain phenomenon. Once just the foundation for cryptocurrencies, blockchain technology has broadened its reach far beyond finance. Today, it plays a role in supply chain management, voting systems, and digital identity verification, among others. However, the decentralized and often anonymous nature of blockchain transactions creates real challenges for regulators. Current laws may not cover the unique features of this technology, leading to gaps that could stifle innovation or leave consumers at risk. The big question is: how can regulations adapt to this new decentralized landscape while still providing the protections that people need?

In the realm of biotechnology, tools like CRISPR gene editing have opened up incredible medical possibilities but also raised ethical and safety concerns. Changing genetic material has serious implications, and the regulations that oversee these technologies must consider the ethical dilemmas they create. While strict regulations might slow down progress, a lack of oversight could lead to risks that impact public health and safety. Finding the right balance between encouraging biotechnological innovation and maintaining high safety standards highlights the urgent need for regulations that can evolve.

Flexibility in regulations is a key principle in this changing landscape. For regulations to be effective, they need to change in real-time based on new information, technological advancements, and input from various stakeholders. There are examples where flexible regulatory approaches have led to positive changes, allowing innovation to thrive while also protecting consumers. One such example is the use of regulatory sandboxes, where startups can test their new ideas in a controlled setting with guidance from regulatory bodies. These sandboxes not only encourage experimentation but also provide valuable insights into how regulations can adjust to new market conditions.

Consider the rise of fintech, which has exploded in recent years. Traditional financial regulations, created for brick-and-mortar banks, often find it hard to keep up with the fast-paced changes in digital financial services. By incorporating flexible regulatory approaches like sandboxes, regulators can observe how new fintech solutions work in practice, assessing risks and benefits before implementing wider regulations. This strategy fosters innovation while keeping consumer protection as a top priority.

Ongoing evaluation and the establishment

of feedback loops are crucial in today's regulatory environment. Regulations shouldn't be set in stone; they need to be viewed as living frameworks that require constant review and improvement. Encouraging a culture of feedback—where industry players, consumers, and regulators communicate openly—can help create responsive regulatory systems. When policymakers actively seek input from those affected by regulations, they can better grasp the real-world effects of their rules and adjust them to meet society's changing needs.

This focus on continuous assessment isn't just an idea; it's backed by real-world examples. For instance, the European Union's General Data Protection Regulation (GDPR) has gone through several reviews since it was put into place in 2018. Feedback from businesses and consumers has led to changes aimed at clearing up confusion and tackling compliance issues. This ongoing process shows how valuable it is to stay open to change and highlights the importance of working together with stakeholders.

As we consider the relationship between innovation and regulation, it's vital to address the ethical issues that come up. The speed of innovation often outpaces regulators' ability to tackle the ethical concerns associated with new technologies. When regulations are created without enough attention to ethical implications, the potential for harm rises significantly. For instance, AI-driven algorithms used in decision-making can raise issues around bias, fairness, and transparency. If regulators focus solely on compliance and ignore ethical principles, they risk perpetuating inequalities and eroding public trust.

Given this, it's clear that ethical considerations should be part of the regulatory process right from the start. Regulations shouldn't just react to issues; they should actively address the ethical impacts of new technologies. Policymakers need to involve ethicists, industry experts, and community members in shaping the regulatory landscape. By taking a multidisciplinary approach to regulation, we can ensure that the public's interests are prioritized and that innovations have a positive impact on society.

The message for policymakers, industry leaders, and the public is straightforward: we need to come together to create a regulatory environment where innovation and protection can work hand in hand. The challenges we face today require us to think differently about regulation. By embracing adaptability, flexibility, and ethical considerations, we can create a future where innovation isn't held back by red tape but instead guided by thoughtful regulations.

Building an effective regulatory framework won't be without its challenges. As we've seen, finding the right balance between promoting innovation and protecting public interests is a tough job. However, by focusing on collaboration among all stakeholders and incorporating continuous assessment, we can begin to tackle the complexities of our ever-evolving world. The responsibility falls on all of us—policymakers, industry leaders, consumers, and advocates—to engage in this important conversation.

As we confront emerging technologies, we need to stay alert and proactive in our regulatory approach. The stakes are high, and mistakes can have serious consequences. But with a commitment to learning and a focus on ethics, we can chart a course that benefits everyone. It's not just about following regulations; it's about building a system that nurtures innovation while protecting the public good.

Looking ahead, let's draw inspiration from the potential that comes from collaboration and adaptability. By creating a regulatory environment that grows alongside technology, we can tap into the full power of innovation while ensuring that it serves the needs of society as a whole. The future of regulation isn't about hindering progress but about seizing opportunities—a chance to build a world where advancement and protection are not at odds but instead work together to create benefits for all.

www.ingramcontent.com/pod-product-compliance
Lightning Source LLC
Chambersburg PA
CBHW052356220526
45465CB00003BB/1125